Classical Piano Solos for Worship Settings

By Gail Smith

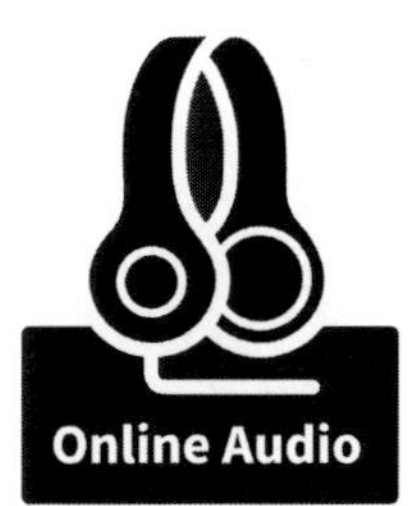

Online Audio

www.melbay.com/94672MEB

AF326904

AUDIO DOWNLOAD CONTENTS

1 Morning Prayer	11 Descend On Us, Holy Spirit	21 To A Wild Rose
2 Sonata For Sunday	12 The Living Water	22 Prelude In A
3 At Peace	13 Song Of Faith	23 Waltz In A
4 Andante	14 Lord Speak To Me	24 Song Without Words
5 A Dream Of Hope	15 Song Of Joy	25 Rejoice
6 Prelude	16 Rest In The Lord	26 Impromptu
7 Sarabande	17 Allemande	27 Promenade
8 Praise The Lord	18 Moments Musicaux	28 O Sacred Head
9 A Kind Thought	19 Pastoral	29 March
10 Consolation	20 Adagio	30 Evening Prayer

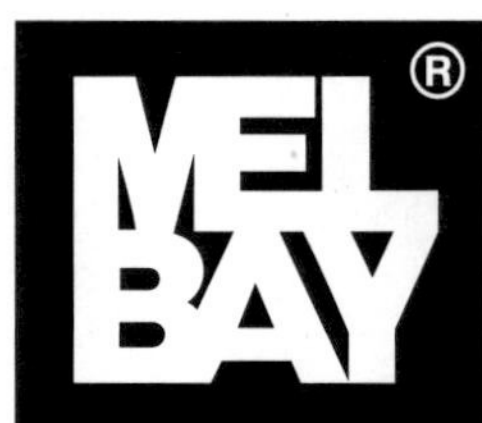

Visit us on the Web at www.melbay.com — E-mail us at email@melbay.com

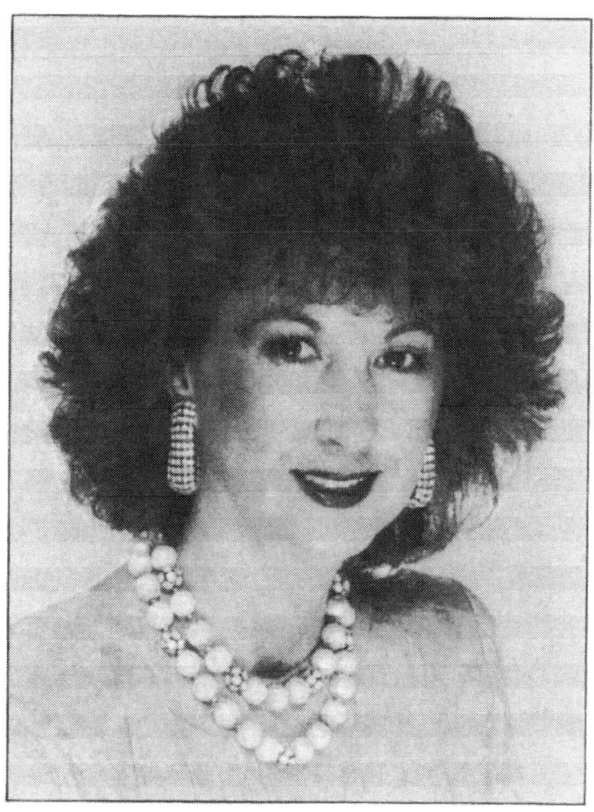

Foreword

Playing the right music at the right time is the key to setting the right mood for each part of the worship service.

I have edited or arranged all of the classical selections in this book so that they are appropriate for church services. The pieces represent different composers, and they all have a certain quality of reverence. Each piece can create a feeling of peace, joy, calmness, love, comfort, and an overall sense of well being for the listener.

It has been said that Music is the language of Heaven and cannot be spoken in words. As you play these beautiful pieces, I pray that you will be uplifted as well as the listeners.

Johann Sebastian Bach, the greatest composer and church musician the world has known, said: "The notes don't disappear . . . but they ascend to the very throne of God as praise too deep for utterance."

Gail

Table Of Contents*

1. **Morning Prayer**
   Cornelius Gurlitt
   Op. 101, No. 2 7

2. **Sonata For Sunday**
   Domenico Scarlatti
   Sonata Longo 358 8

3. **At Peace**
   E. Granados
   Op. 5, No. 5 10

4. **Andante**
   Christoph Willibald von Gluck
   from Orpheus 11

5. **A Dream Of Hope**
   Robert Schumann
   Op. 15, No. 7 12

6. **Prelude**
   Jean Sibelius
   Op. 24, No. 9 13

7. **Sarabande**
   George Frederic Handel 14

8. **Praise The Lord**
   W. A. Mozart
   excerpt from Sonata 6, K284 16

9. **A Kind Thought**
   Ludwig van Beethoven
   Minuet 18

10. **Consolation**
    Felix Mendelssohn
    Op. 30, No. 3 19

11. **Descend On Us, Holy Spirit**
    W. A. Mozart
    excerpt from Sonata No. 3, K281 20

12. **The Living Water**
    Stephen Heller
    Op. 45 22

13. **Song Of Faith**
    Johann Kuhnau
    from Biblical Sonata No. 5 24

14. **Lord Speak To Me**
    Robert Schumann
    Op. 23, No. 4 26

15. **Song Of Joy**
    Johann Kuhnau
    from Biblical Sonata No. 3 28

16. **Rest In The Lord**
    J. S. Bach
    The Goldberg Variations No. 19 32

17. **Allemande**
    George Frederic Handel
    from Suite No. 14 33

18. **Moments Musicaux**
    Franz Schubert
    Op. 94 34

19. **Pastoral**
    W. A. Mozart
    excerpt from Sonata K331 37

20. **Adagio**
    Ludwig van Beethoven
    from Sonata Op. 13 38

21. **To A Wild Rose**
    Edward MacDowell
    Op. 51, No. 1 40

22. **Prelude In A**
    Frederic Chopin
    Op. 28, No. 7 42

23. **Waltz In A**
    J. Brahms
    Op. 39, No. 15 43

24. **Song Without Words**
    Felix Mendelssohn
    Op. 19, No. 4 44

25. **Rejoice**
    Gottlieb Muffat 46

26. **Impromptu**
    Franz Schubert
    excerpt from Sonata Op. 142 49

27. **Promenade**
    Modeste P. Moussorgsky
    from Pictures From An Exhibition 50

28. **O Sacred Head**
    Johann Kuhnau
    from Biblical Sonata No. 4 52

29. **March**
    G. Meyerbeer
    from Le Prophete 54

30. **Evening Prayer**
    Engelbert Humperdinck
    from Hansel And Gretel 55

*An alphabetical index of all selections may be found on page 56.

A Listing Of The Contents With Suggested Uses

Prelude

Adagio	Beethoven	38
Allemande	Handel	33
Andante	Gluck	11
At Peace	Granados	10
A Dream Of Hope	Schumann	12
A Kind Thought	Beethoven	18
The Living Water	Heller	22
Lord Speak To Me	Schumann	26
Moments Musicaux	Schumann	34
Morning Prayer	Gurlitt	7
Praise The Lord	Mozart	16
Prelude	Sibelius	13
Promenade	Moussorgsky	50
Rejoice	Muffat	46
Sarabande	Handel	14
Song Of Faith	Kuhnau	24
Song Of Joy	Kuhnau	28
Song Without Words	Mendelssohn	44
To A Wild Rose	MacDowell	40
Waltz In A	Brahms	43

Offertory

Andante	Gluck	11
A Dream Of Hope	Schumann	12
Lord Speak To Me	Schumann	26
Praise The Lord	Mozart	16
Rejoice	Muffat	46
Sarabande	Handel	14
Sonata For Sunday	Scarlatti	8
Song Of Faith	Kuhnau	24
Song Of Joy	Kuhnau	28
Song Without Words	Mendelssohn	44
To A Wild Rose	MacDowell	40

Baptism

Impromptu	Schubert	49
The Living Water	Heller	22
Pastoral	Mozart	37
Prelude In A	Chopin	42
Rest In The Lord	Bach	32
Waltz In A	Brahms	43

Interlude

Impromptu	Schubert	49
A Kind Thought	Beethoven	18
Morning Prayer	Gurlitt	7
Pastoral	Mozart	37
Prelude	Sibelius	13
Prelude In A	Chopin	42
Waltz In A	Brahms	43

Prayer

At Peace	Granados	10
Evening Prayer	Humperdinck	55
A Kind Thought	Beethoven	18
Morning Prayer	Gurlitt	7
Pastoral	Mozart	41
Prelude In A	Chopin	42
Rest In The Lord	Bach	32

Postlude

Allemande	Handel	33
March	Meyerbeer	54
Promenade	Moussorgsky	50
Rejoice	Muffat	46
Song Of Faith	Kuhnau	24
Song Of Joy	Kuhnau	28

Communion

At Peace	Granados	10
A Kind Thought	Beethoven	18
Morning Prayer	Gurlitt	7
Pastoral	Mozart	37
Prelude In A	Chopin	42
Rest In The Lord	Bach	32

A Listing Of The Contents By Composer

J. S. Bach
Rest In The Lord *(The Goldberg Variations No. 19)* 32

Ludwig van Beethoven
Adagio *(from Sonata Op. 13)* 38
A Kind Thought *(Minuet)* 18

J. Brahms
Waltz In A *(Op. 39, No. 15)* 43

Frederic Chopin
Prelude In A *(Op. 28, No. 7)* 42

Christoph Willibald von Gluck
Andante *(from Orpheus)* 11

E. Granados
At Peace *(Op. 5, No. 5)* 10

Cornelius Gurlitt
Morning Prayer *(Op. 101, No. 2)* 7

George Frederic Handel
Allemande *(from Suite No. 14)* 33
Sarabande 14

Stephen Heller
The Living Water *(Op. 45)* 22

Engelbert Humperdinck
Evening Prayer *(from Hansel And Gretel)* 55

Johann Kuhnau
O Sacred Head *(from Biblical Sonata No. 4)* 52
Song Of Faith *(from Biblical Sonata No. 5)* 24
Song Of Joy *(from Biblical Sonata No. 3)* 28

Edward MacDowell
To A Wild Rose *(Op. 51, No. 1)* 40

Felix Mendelssohn
Consolation *(Op. 30, No. 3)* 19
Song Without Words *(Op. 19, No. 4)* 44

G. Meyerbeer
March *(from Le Prophete)* 54

Modeste P. Moussorgsky
Promenade *(from Pictures From An Exhibition)* 50

W. A. Mozart
Descend On Us, Holy Spirit *(excerpt from Sonata No. 3, K281)* 20
Pastoral *(excerpt from Sonata K331)* 37
Praise The Lord *(excerpt from Sonata 6, K284)* .16

Gottlieb Muffat
Rejoice 46

Domenico Scarlatti
Sonata For Sunday *(Sonata Longo 358)* 8

Franz Schubert
Impromptu *(excerpt from Sonata Op. 142)* 49
Moments Musicaux *(Op. 94)* 34

Robert Schumann
A Dream Of Hope *(Op. 15, No. 7)* 12
Lord Speak To Me *(Op. 23, No. 4)* 26

Jean Sibelius
Prelude *(Op. 24, No. 9)* 13

Morning Prayer

Cornelius Gurlitt, Op. 101, No. 2

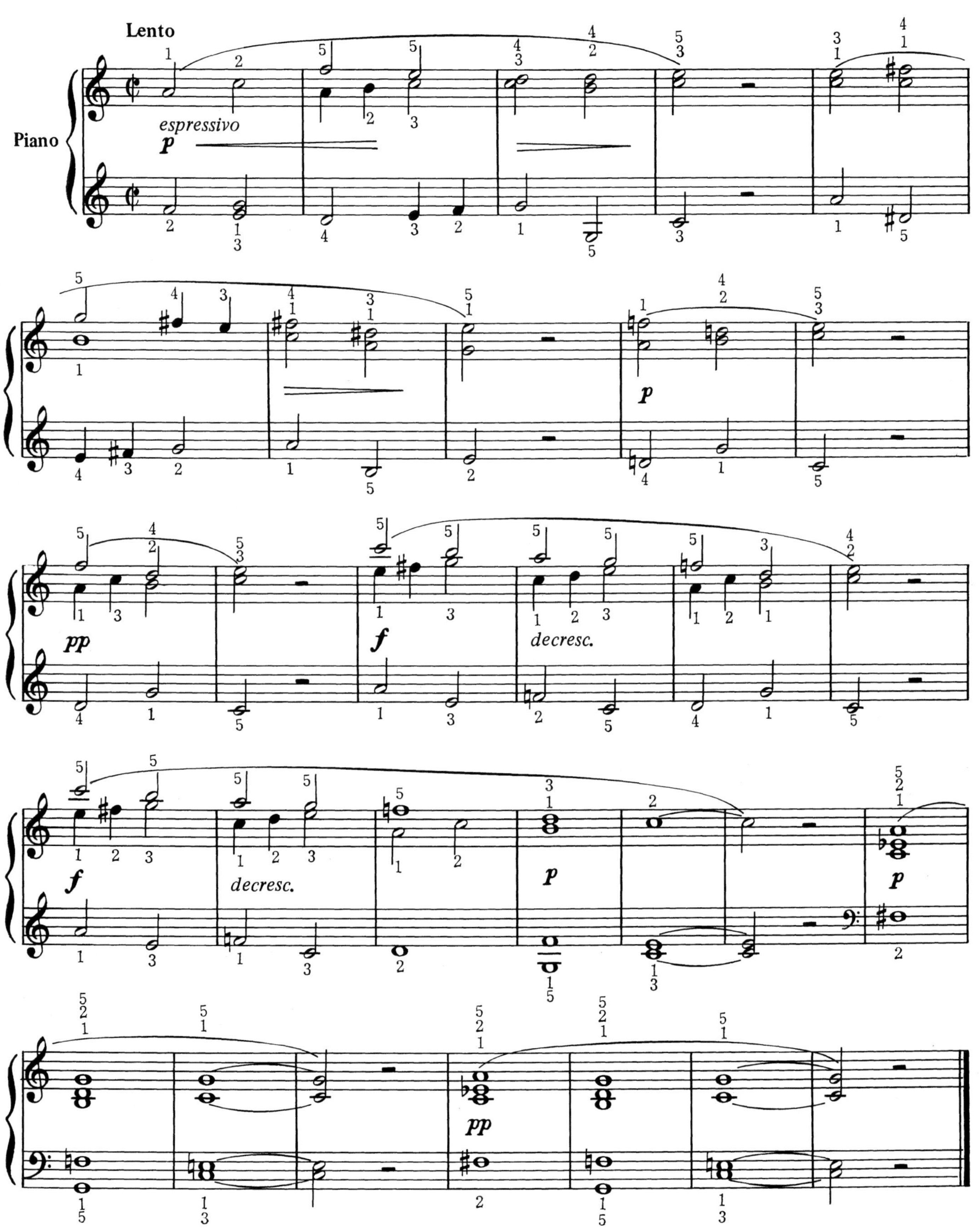

Sonata For Sunday

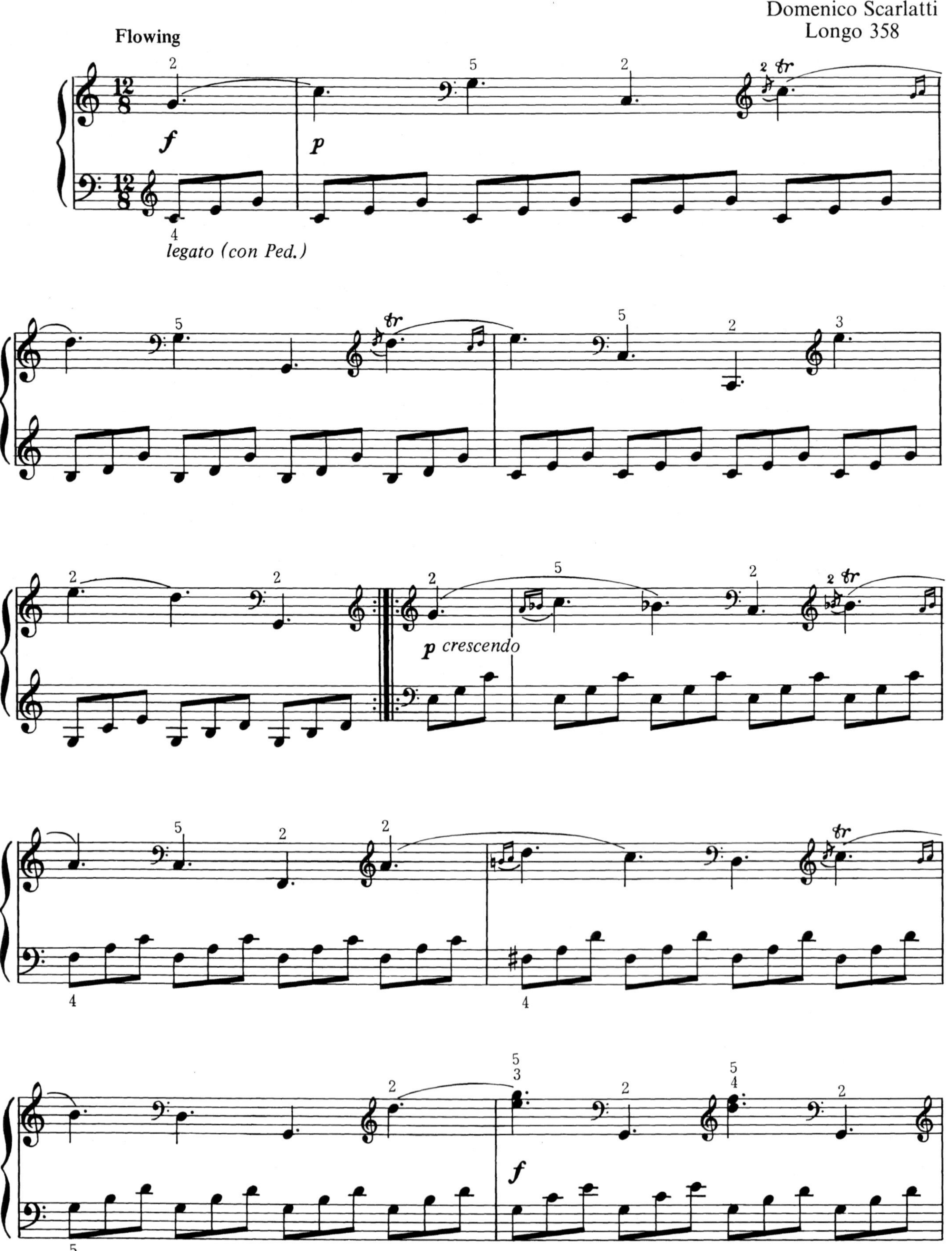

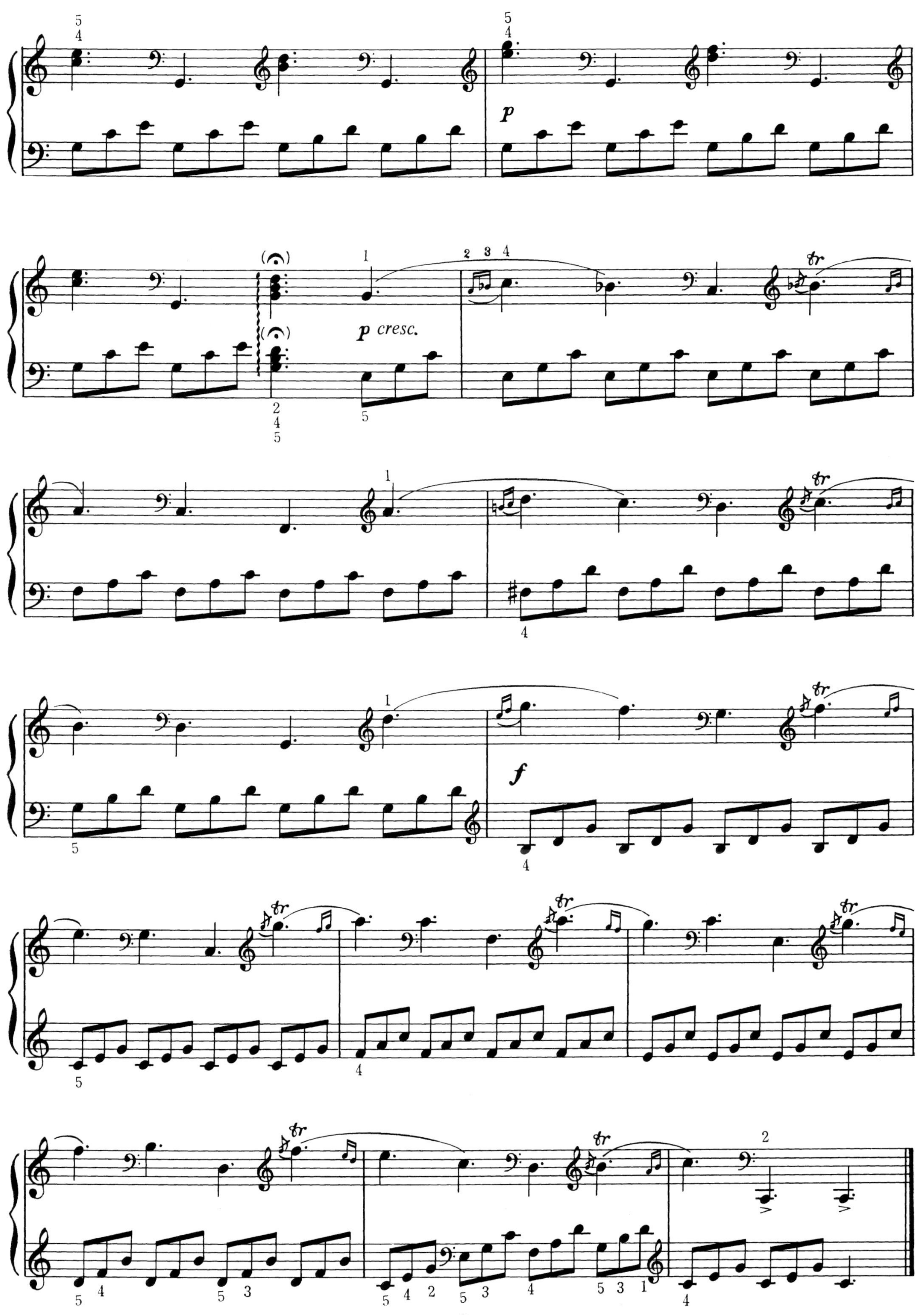
9

At Peace

An excerpt from
Playera by E. Granados
Op. 5, No. 5
Andante
mp
leggiero molto
con molto espressione
f
p
f
p
rit. pp
mp
a tempo
cresc.
decrescendo
rit.
p
molto rit.

Andante
(from "Orpheus")

Christoph Willibald von Gluck
(1714-1787)

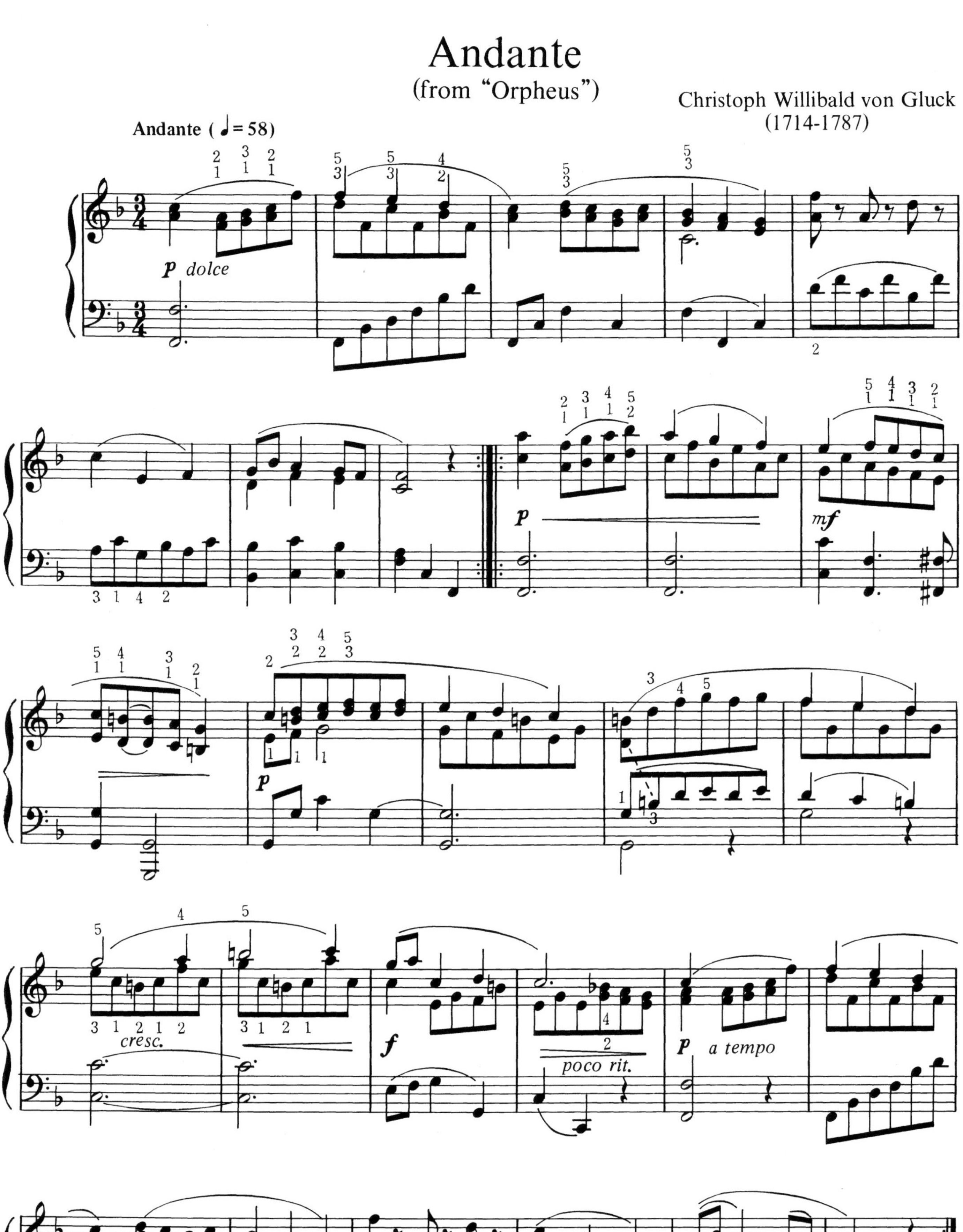

A Dream Of Hope

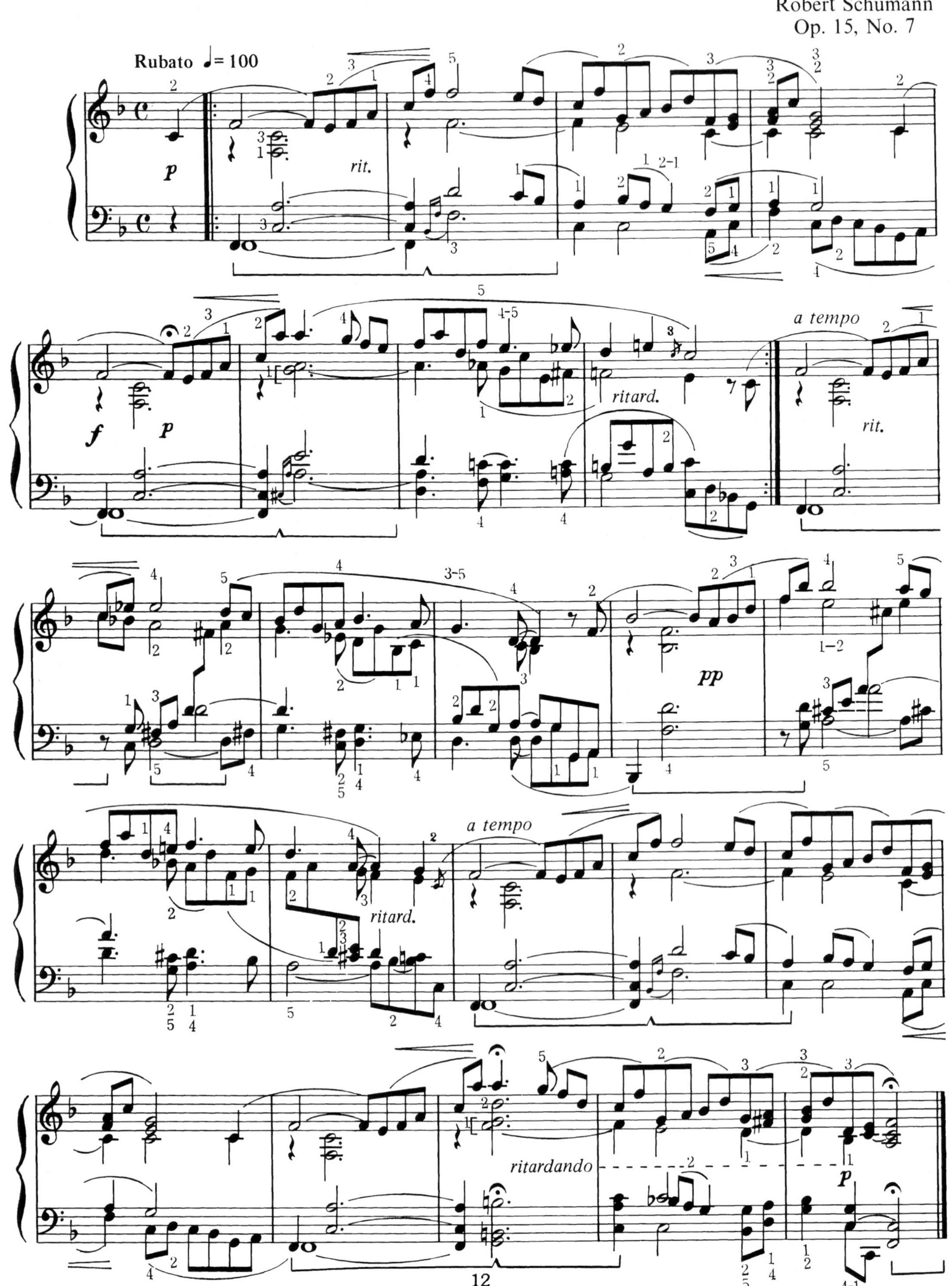

12

Prelude

excerpt from Romance by
Jean Sibelius, Op. 24, No. 9

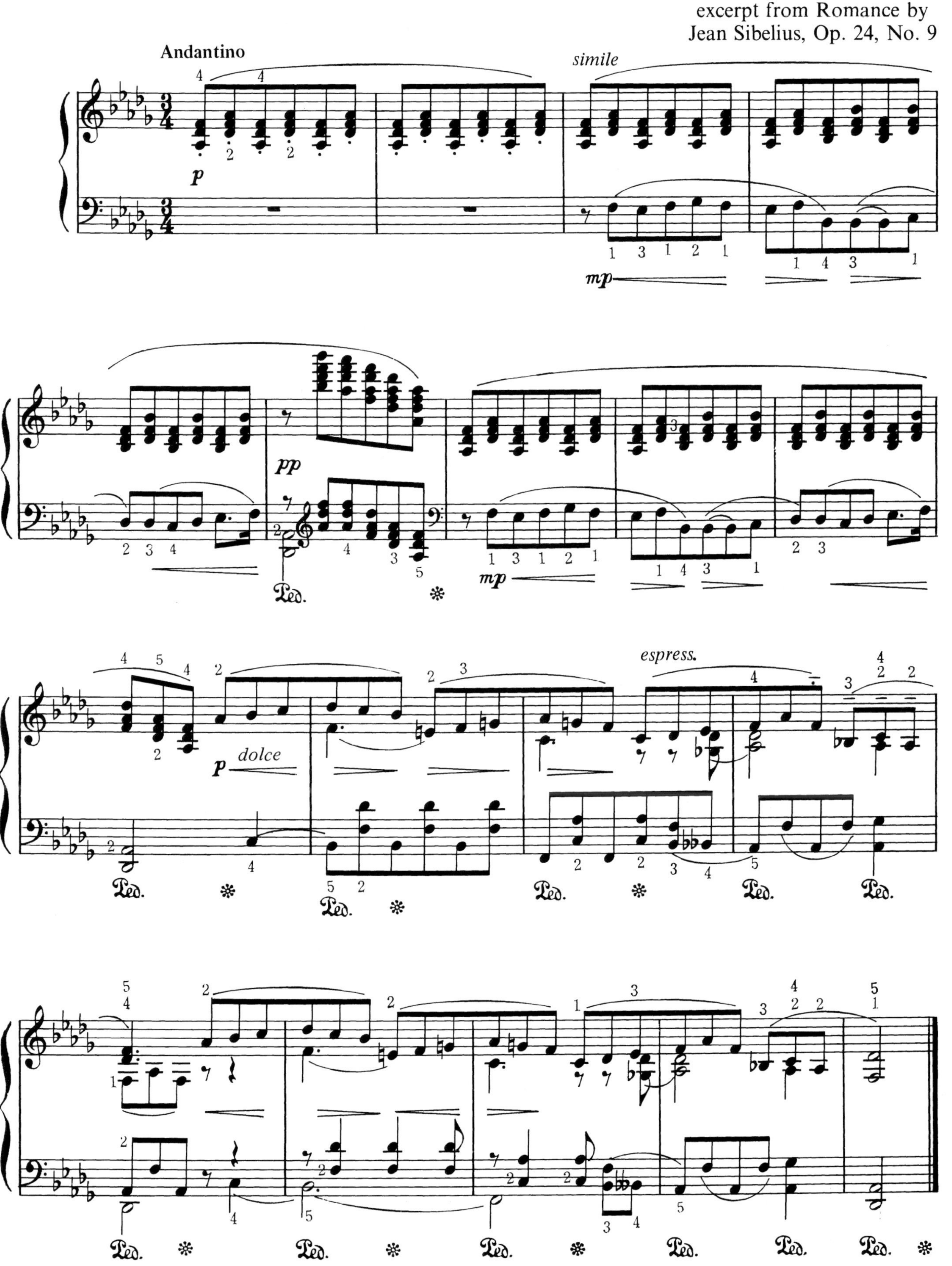

Sarabande

Handel

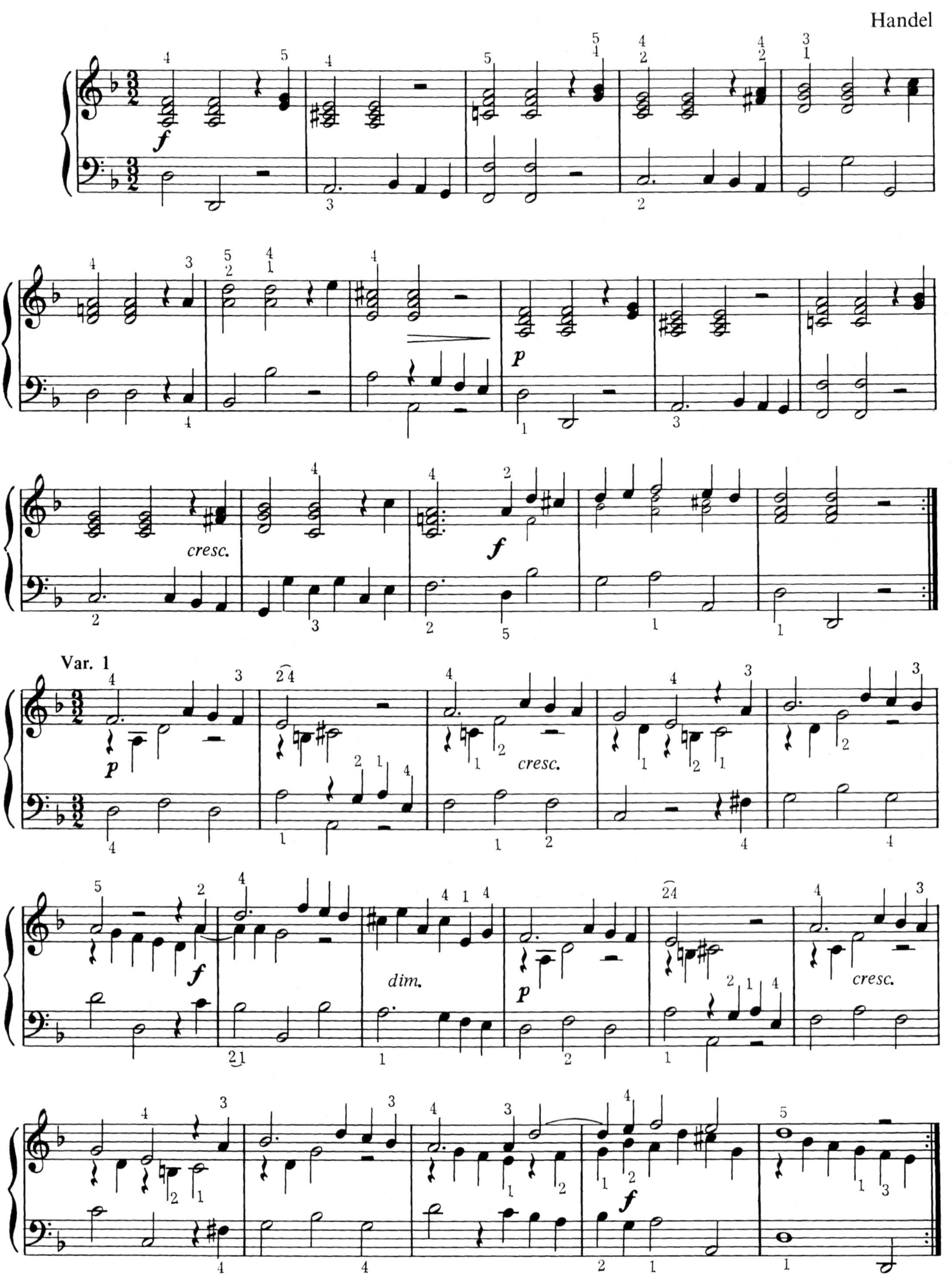

14

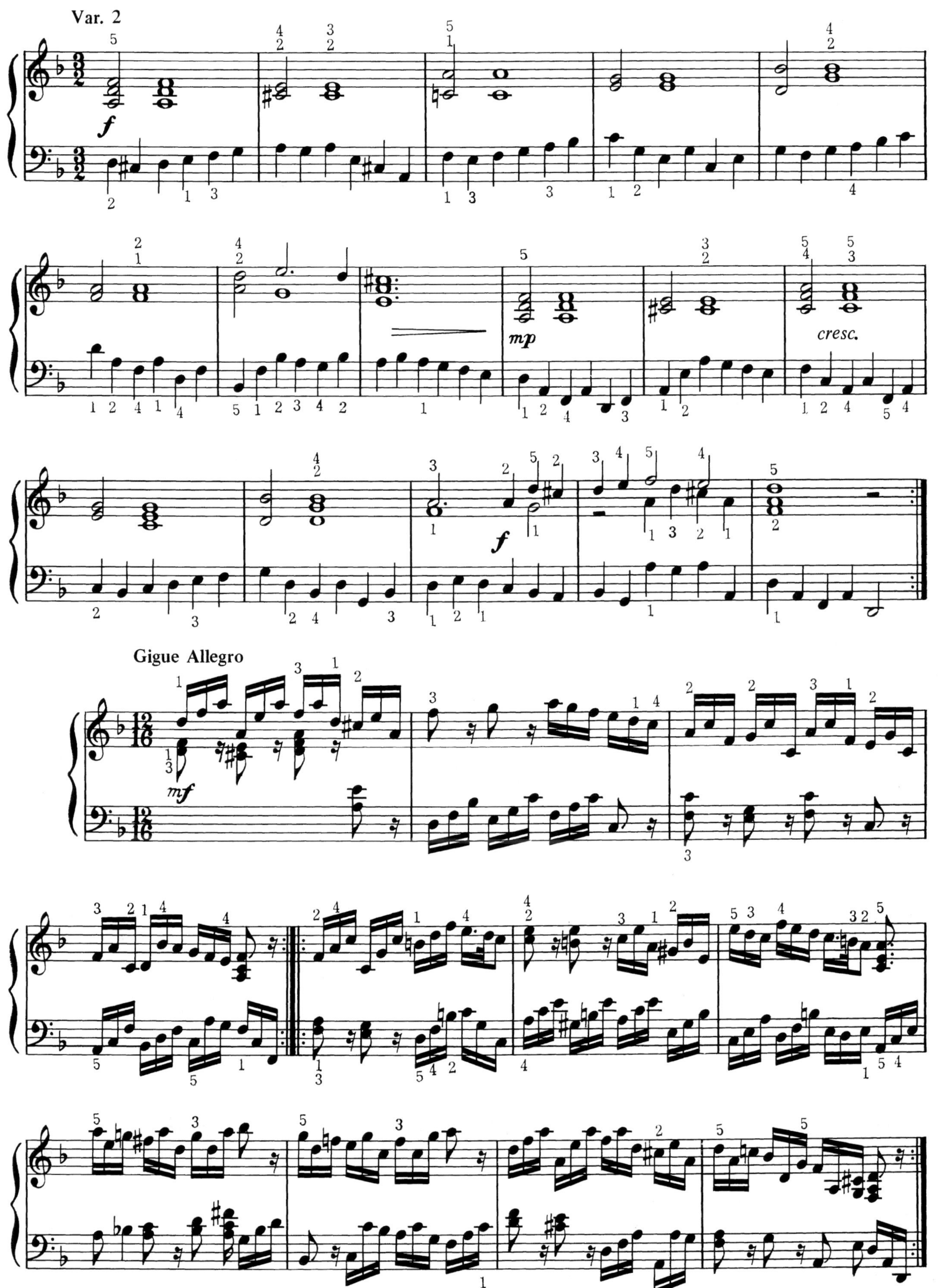

Var. 2
f
mp
cresc.
f
Gigue Allegro
mf

Praise The Lord
(Sonata No. 6, K. 284)
Theme And Variation

Mozart

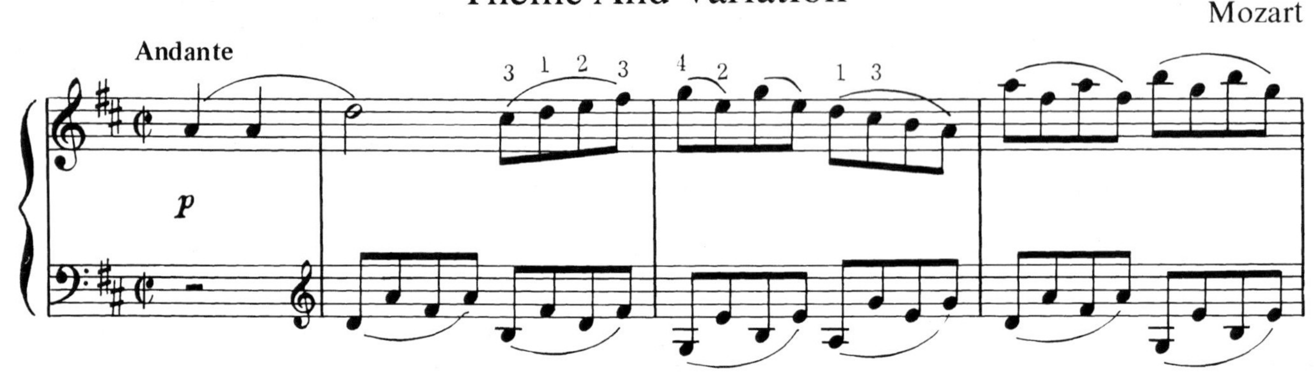

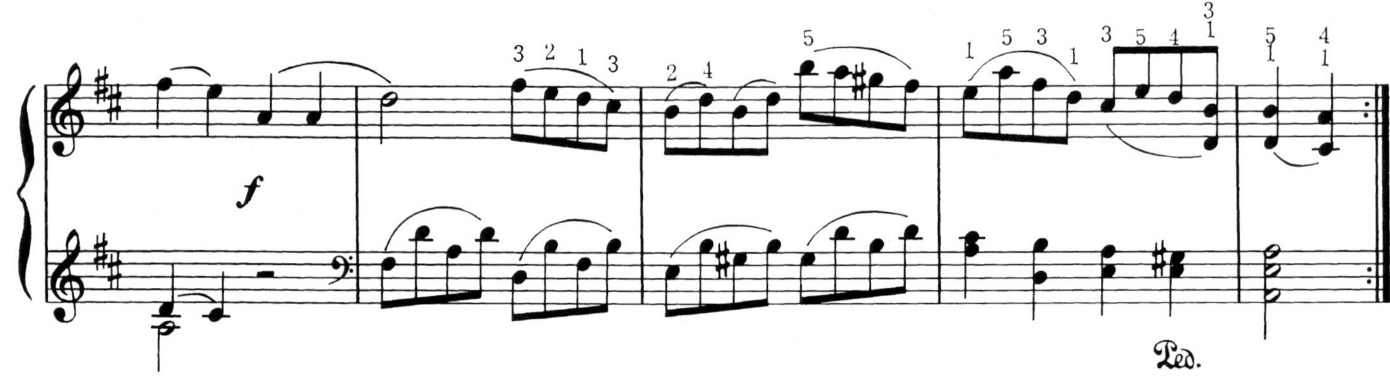

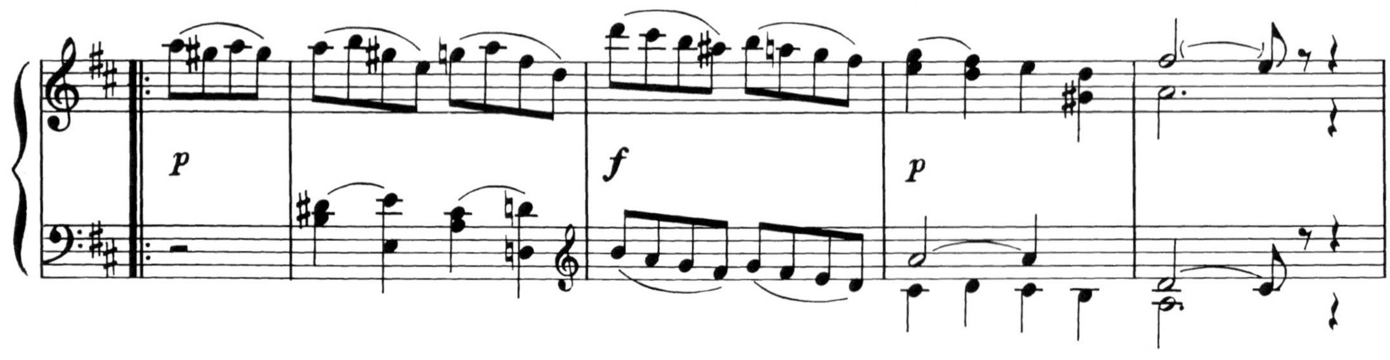

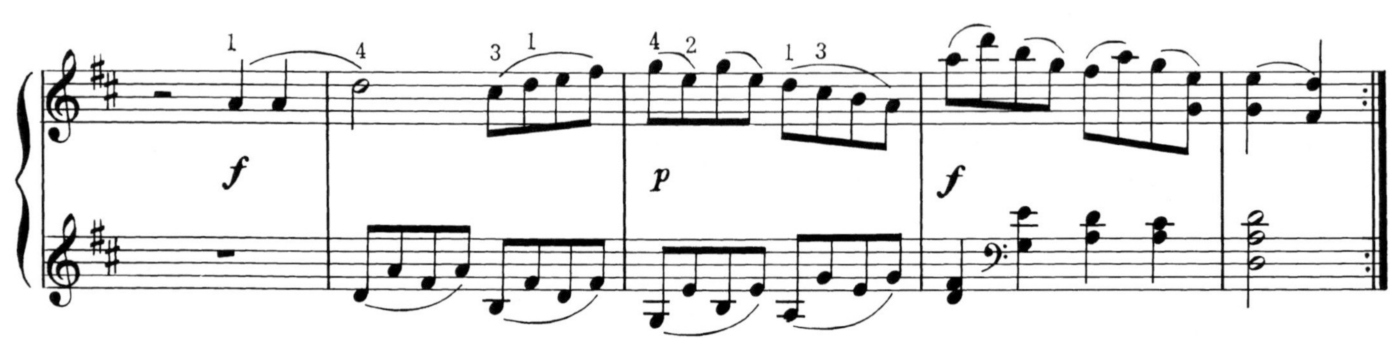

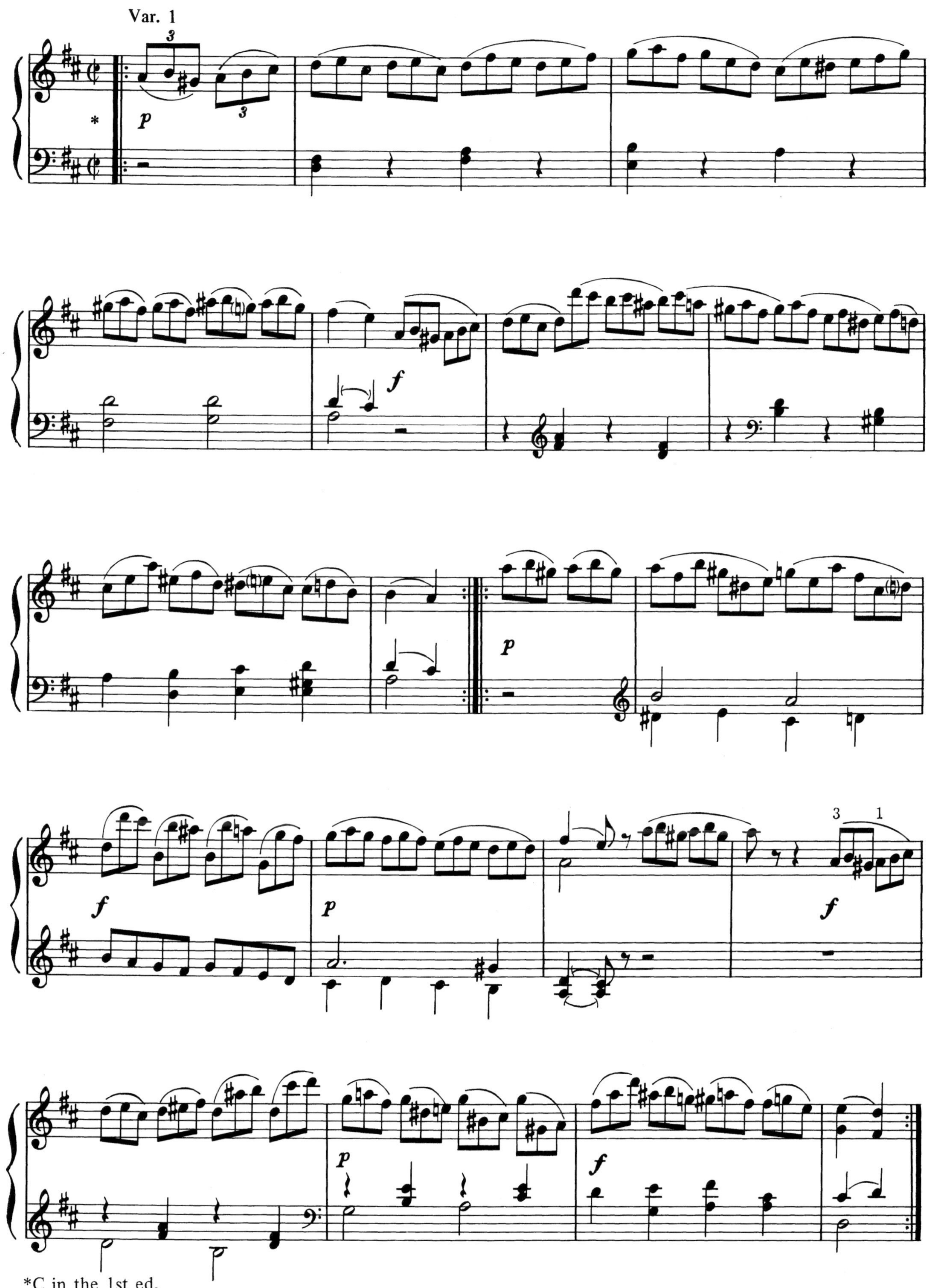

Var. 1
p
*
*C in the 1st ed.

A Kind Thought

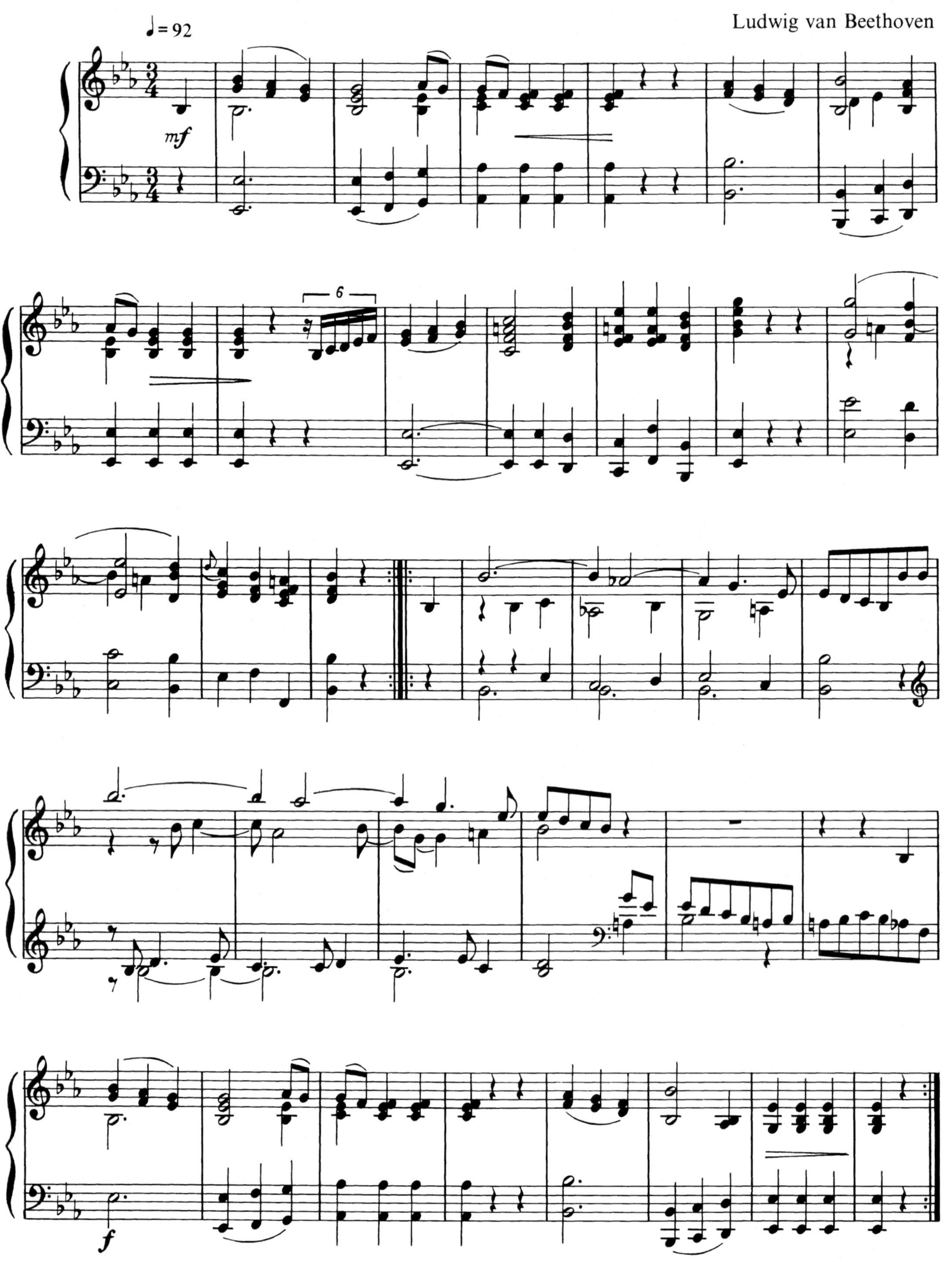

Consolation

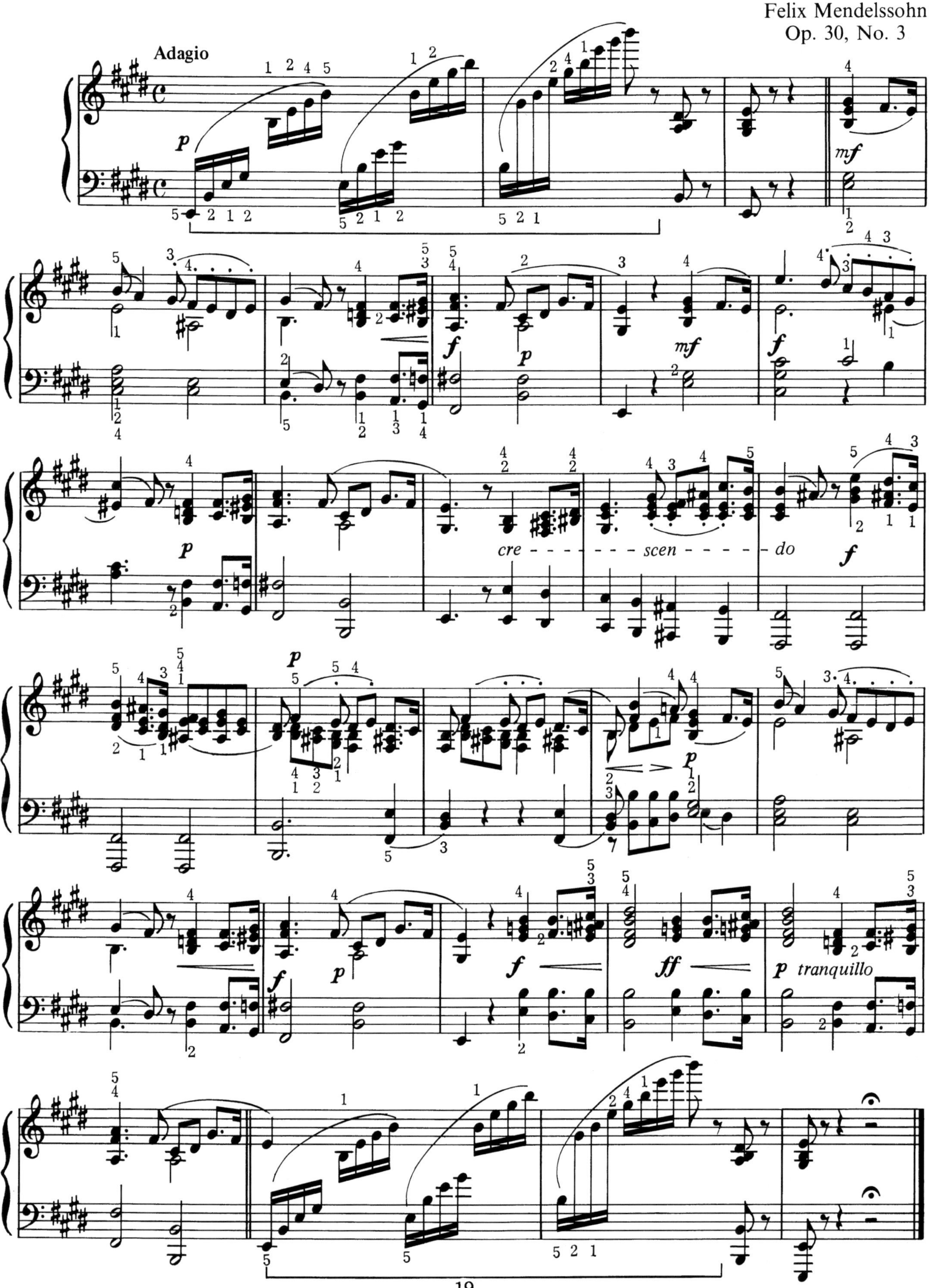

Descend On Us, Holy Spirit

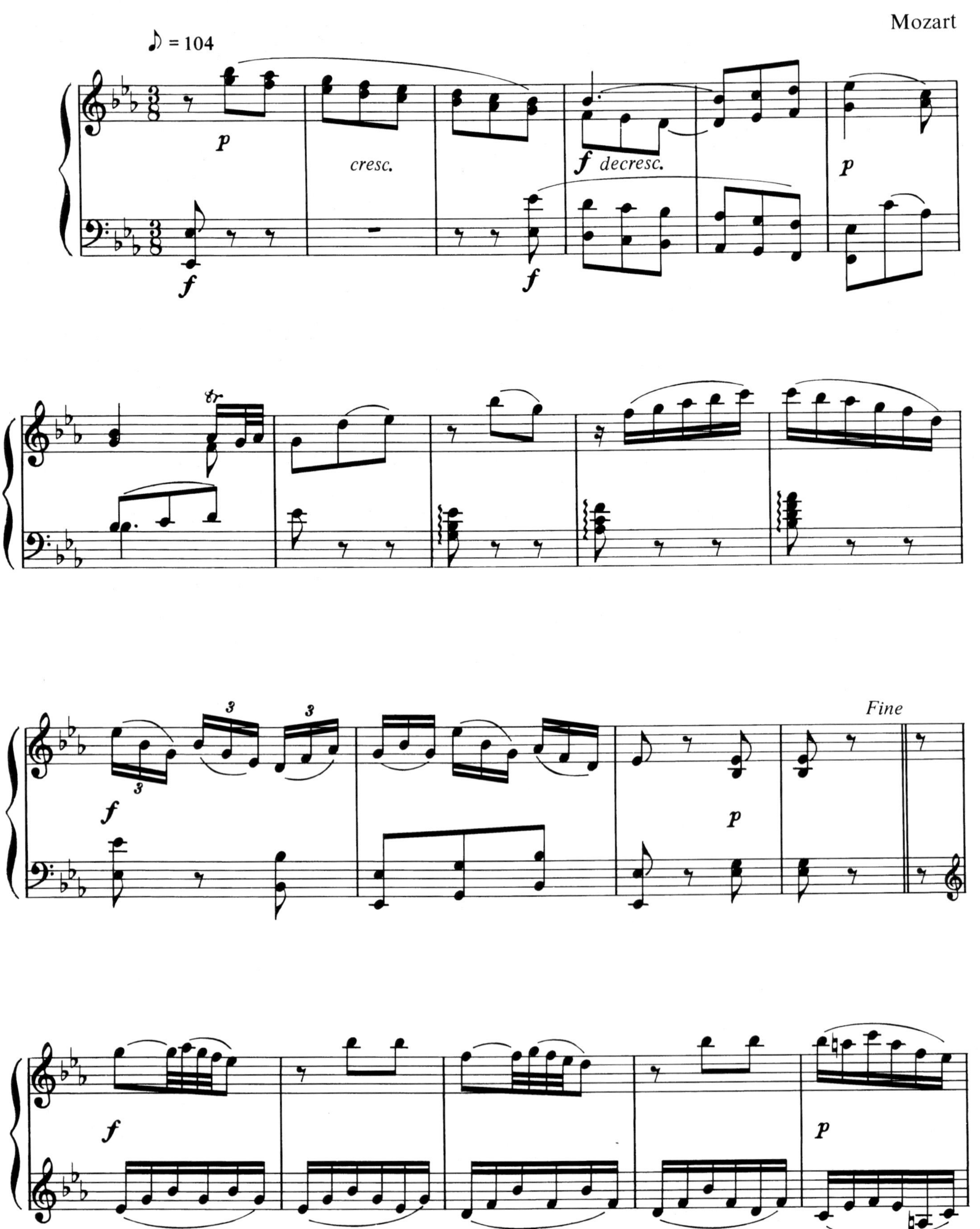

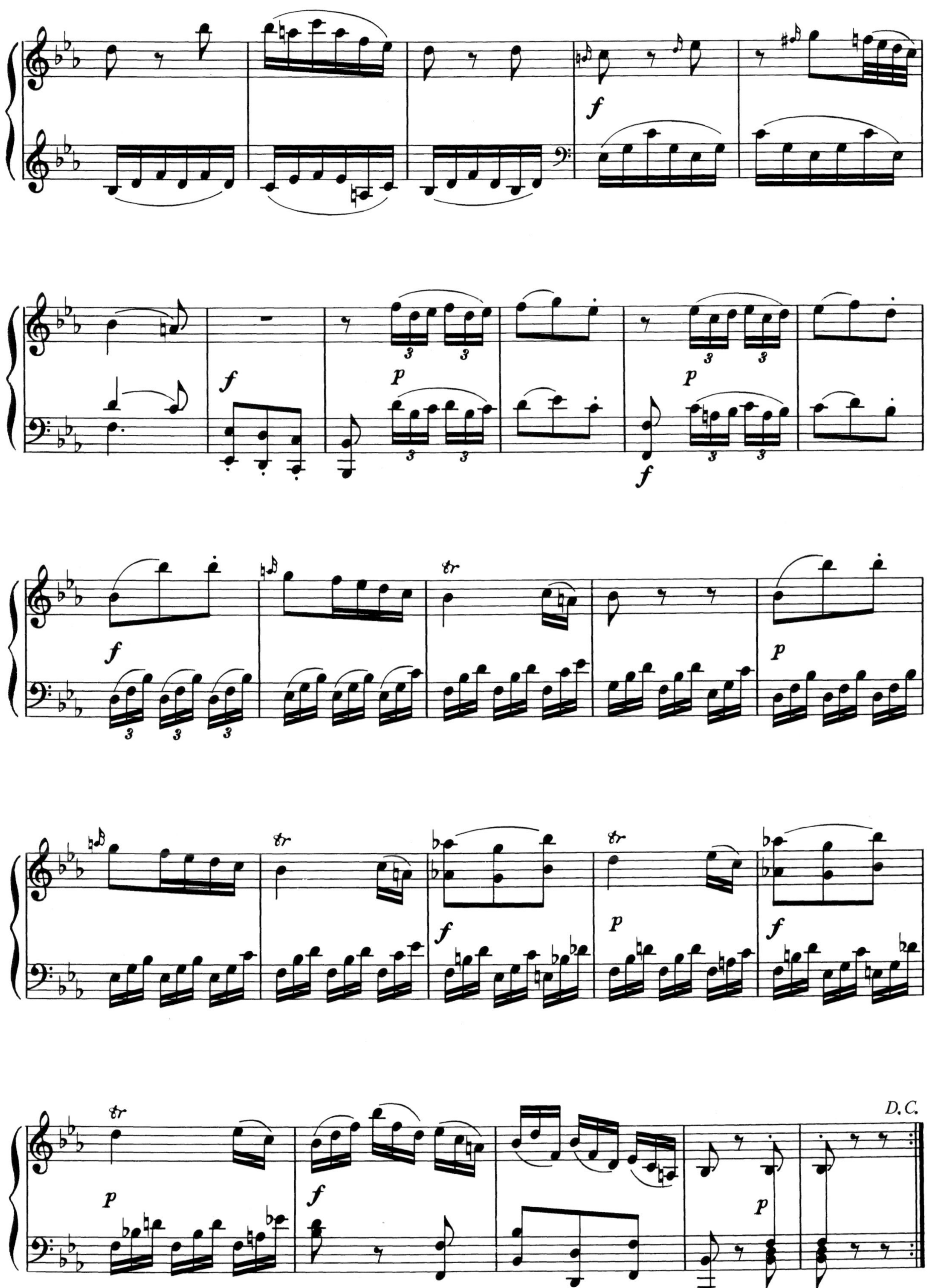

The Living Water

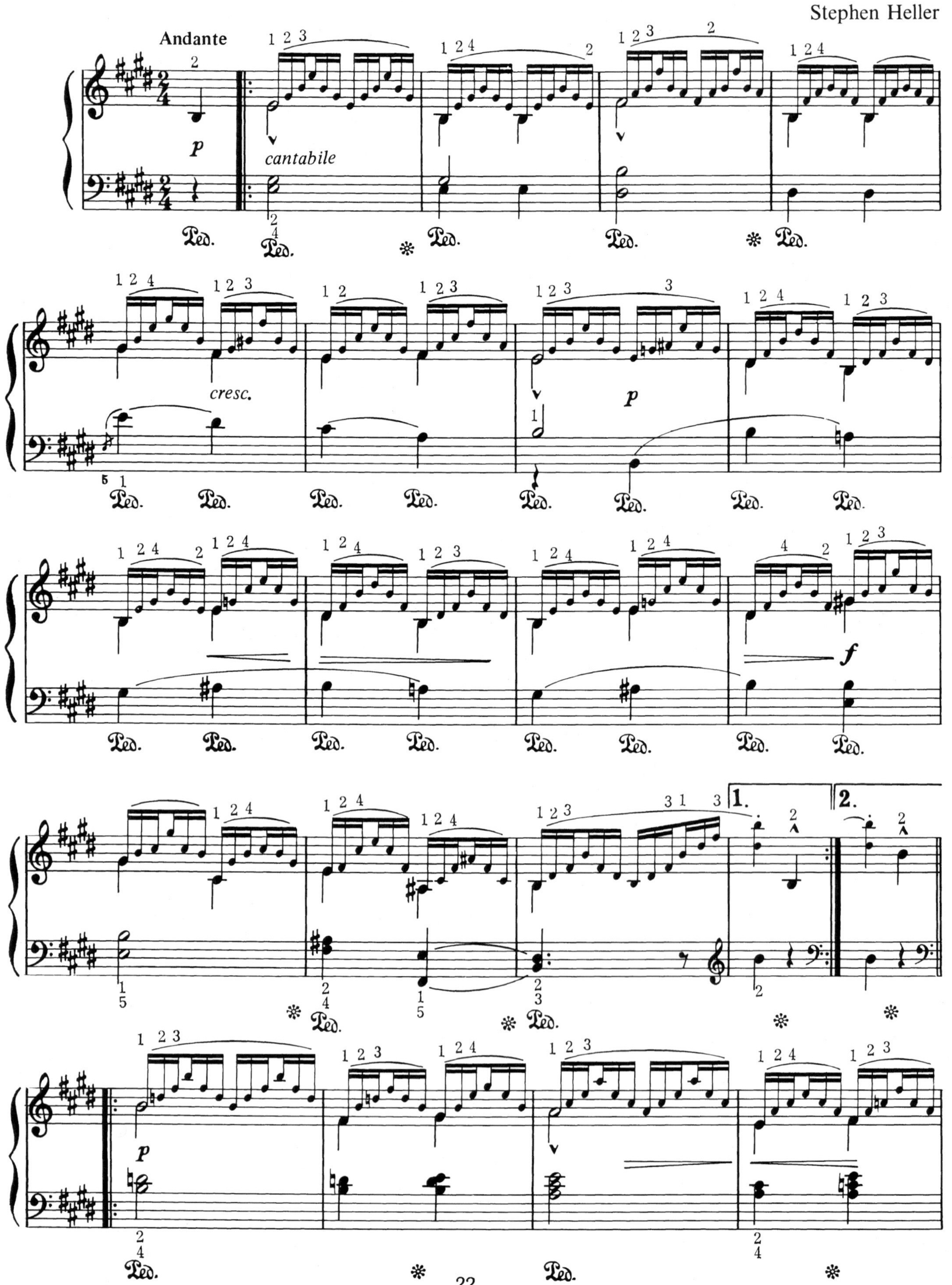

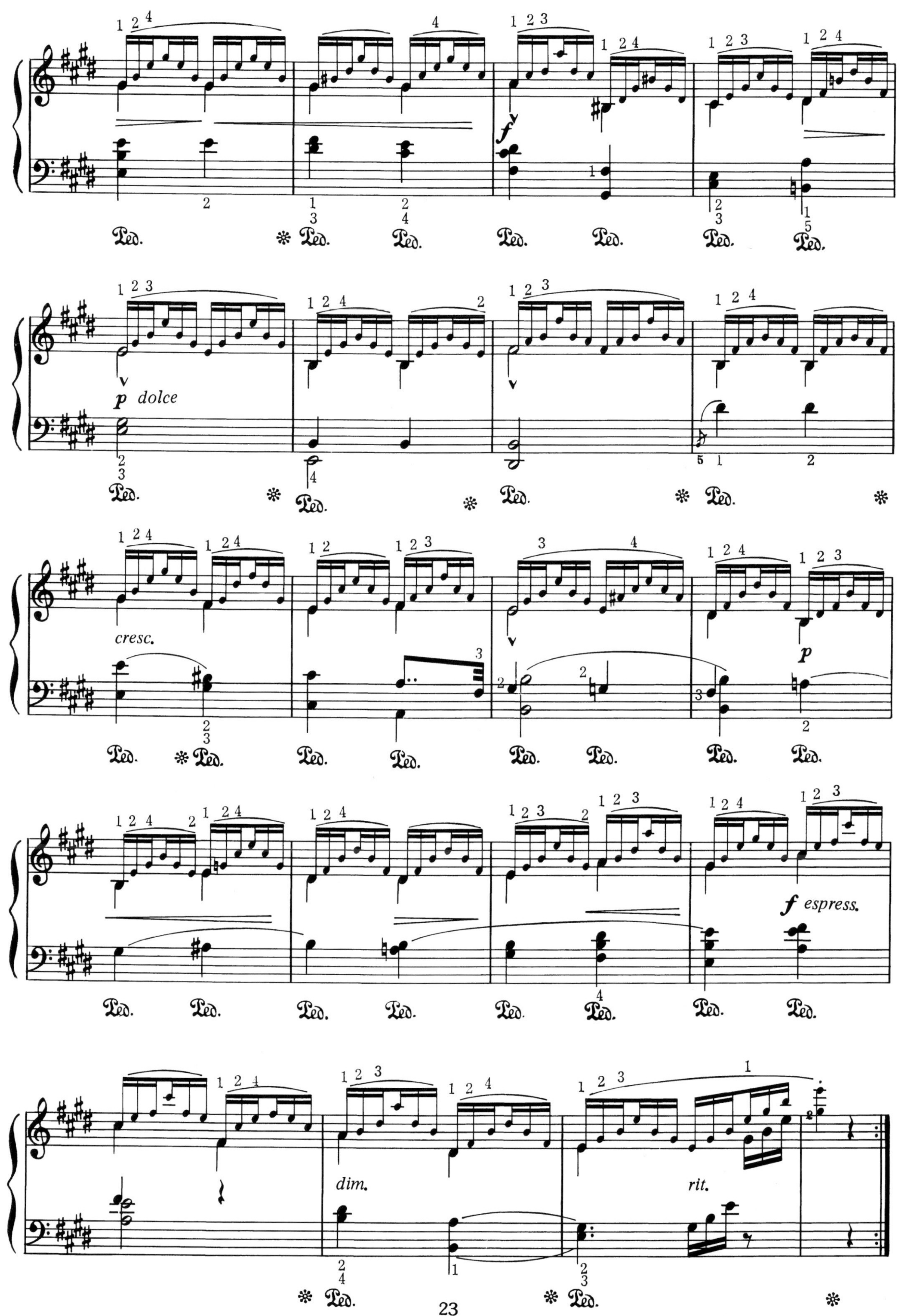

Song Of Faith

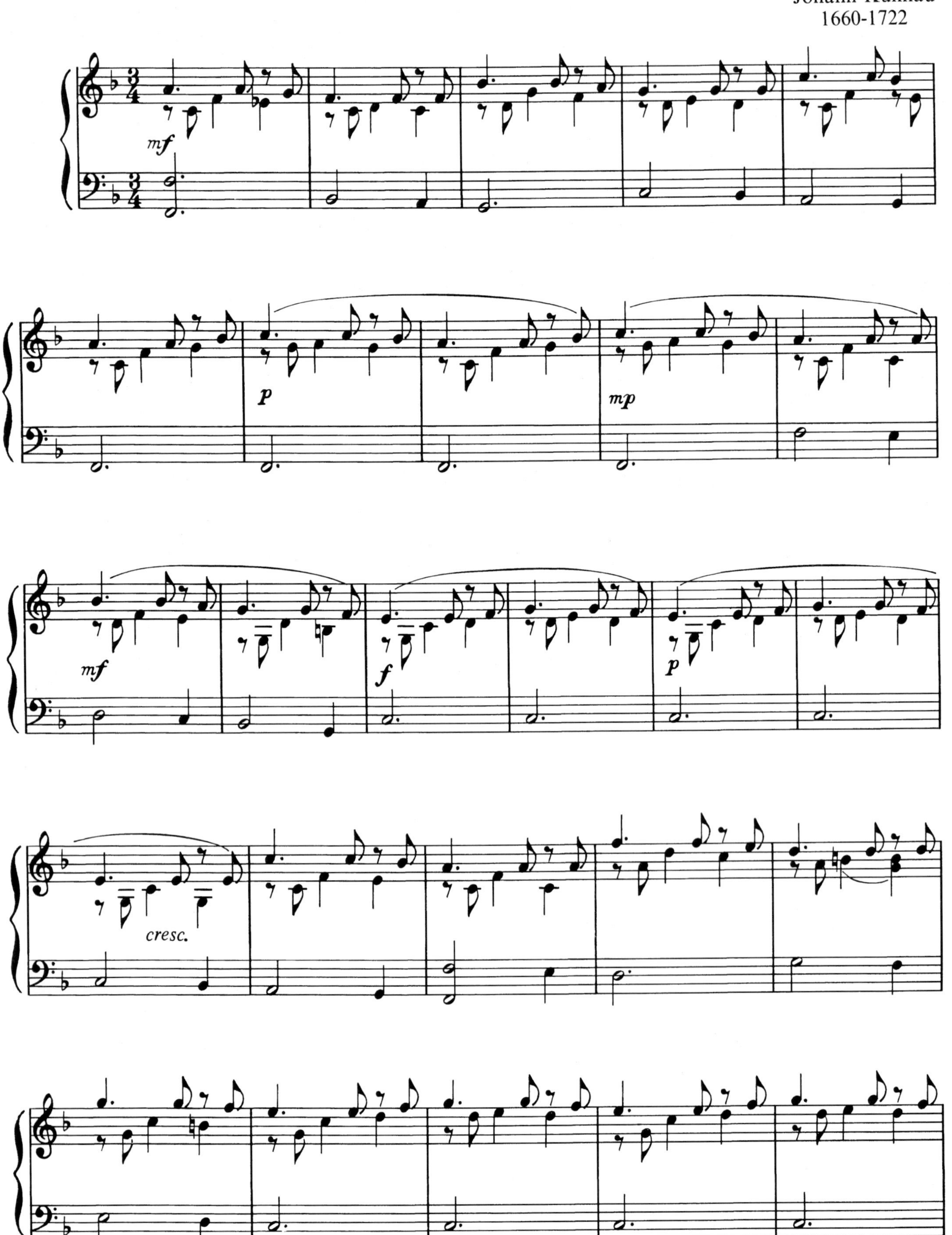

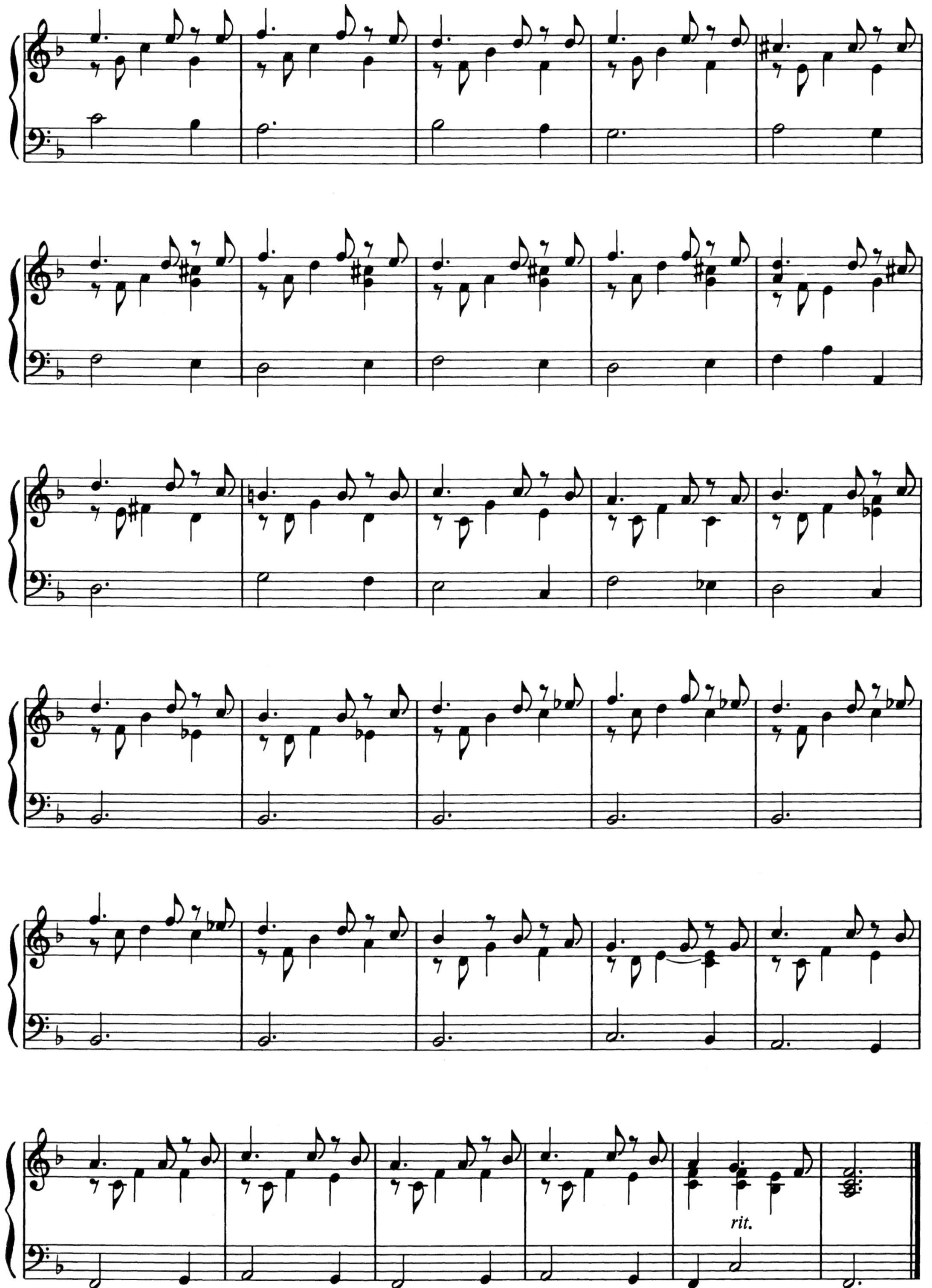
rit.

Lord Speak To Me

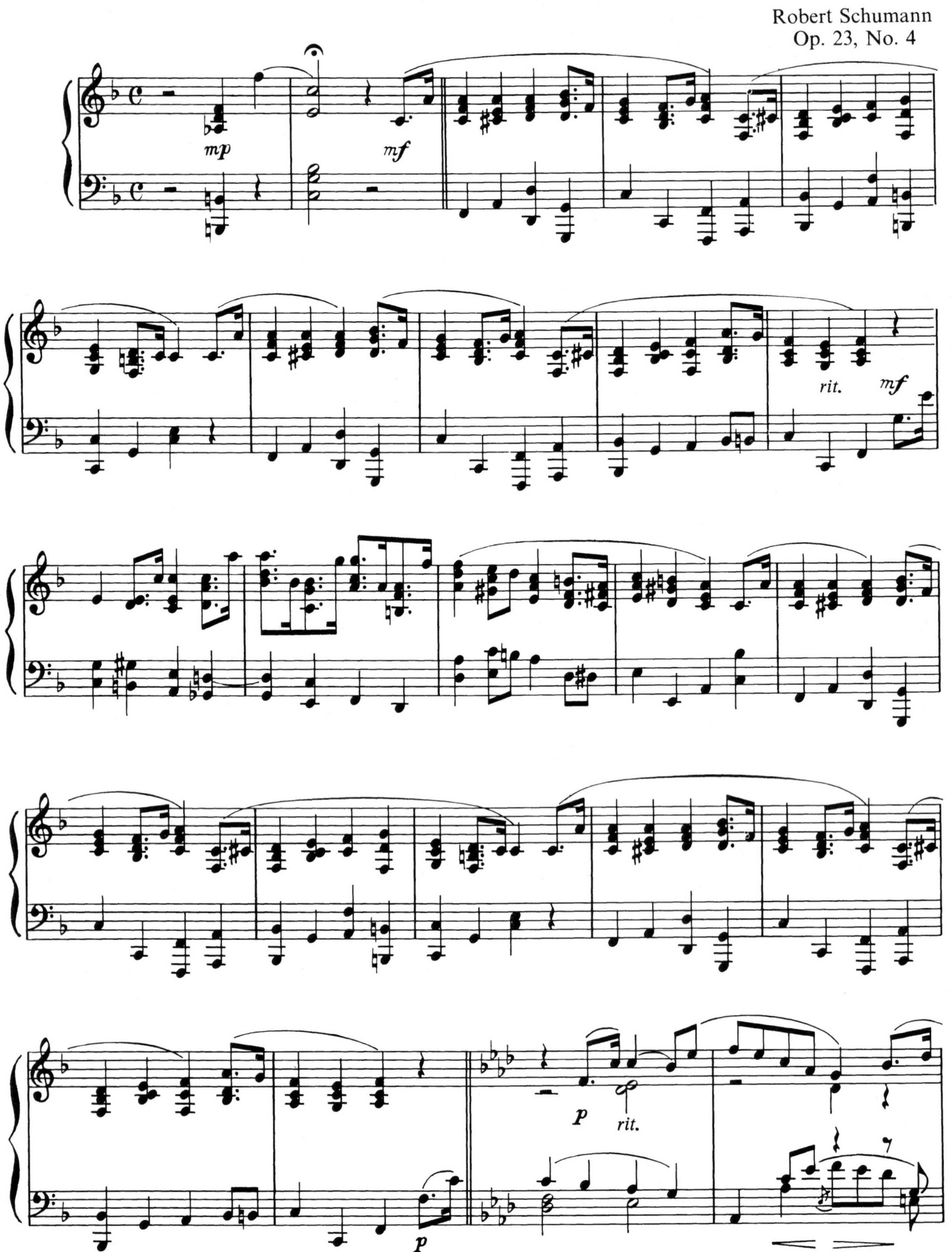

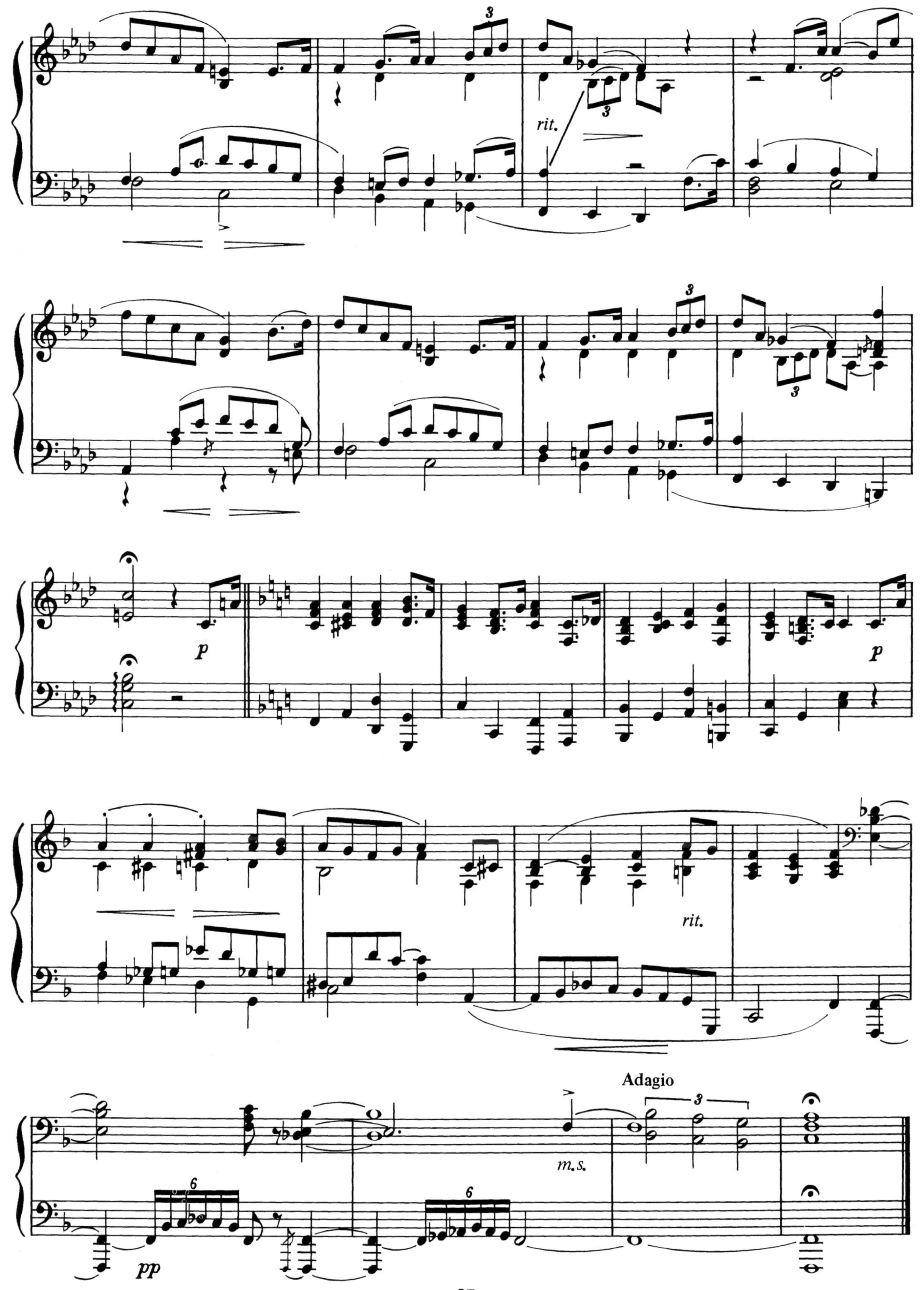

rit.
Adagio
m.s.
p
p
pp

Song Of Joy
(excerpt from Biblical Sonata No. 3)

Johann Kuhnau
1660-1722

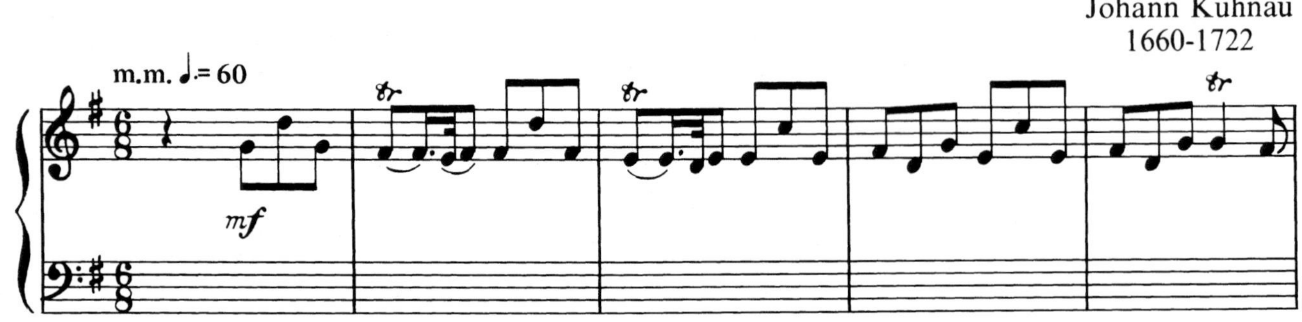

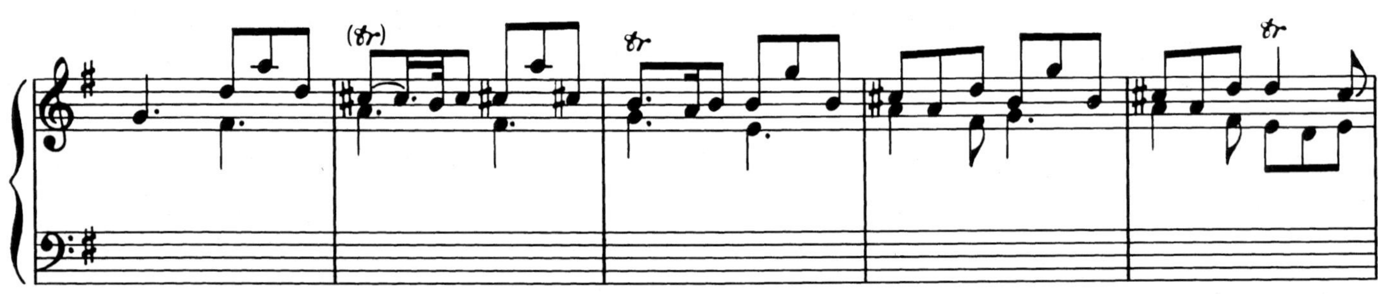

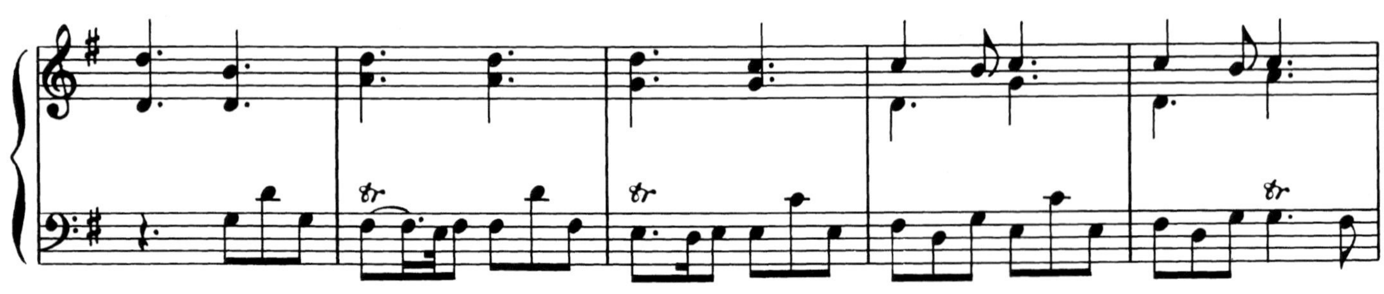

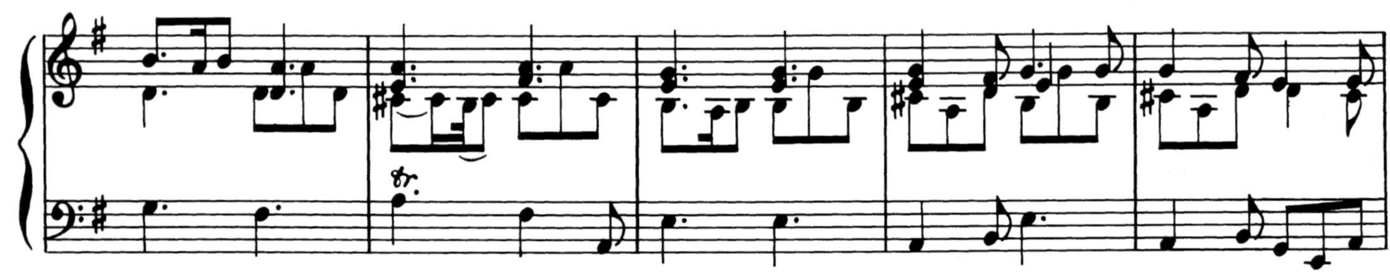

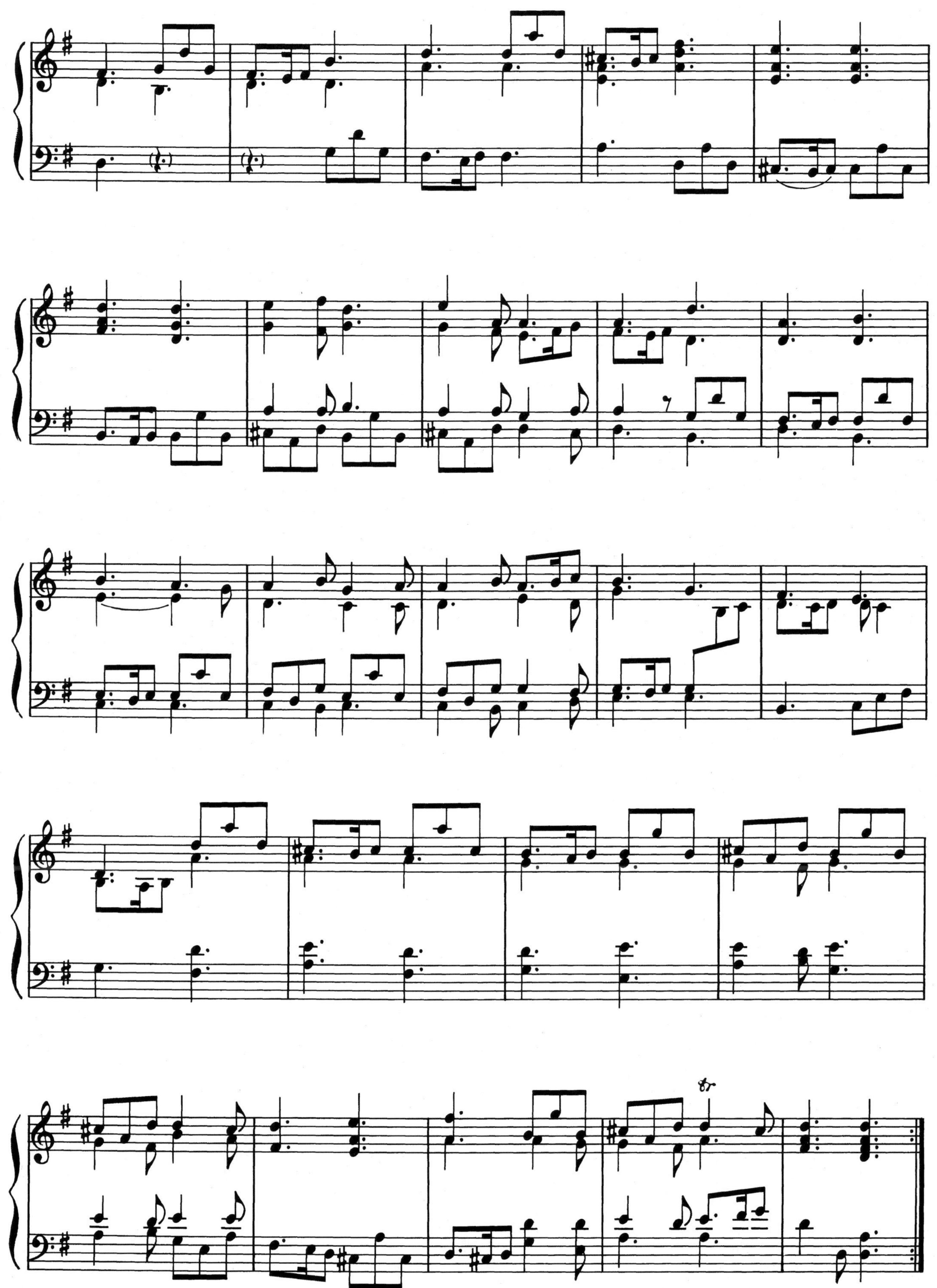

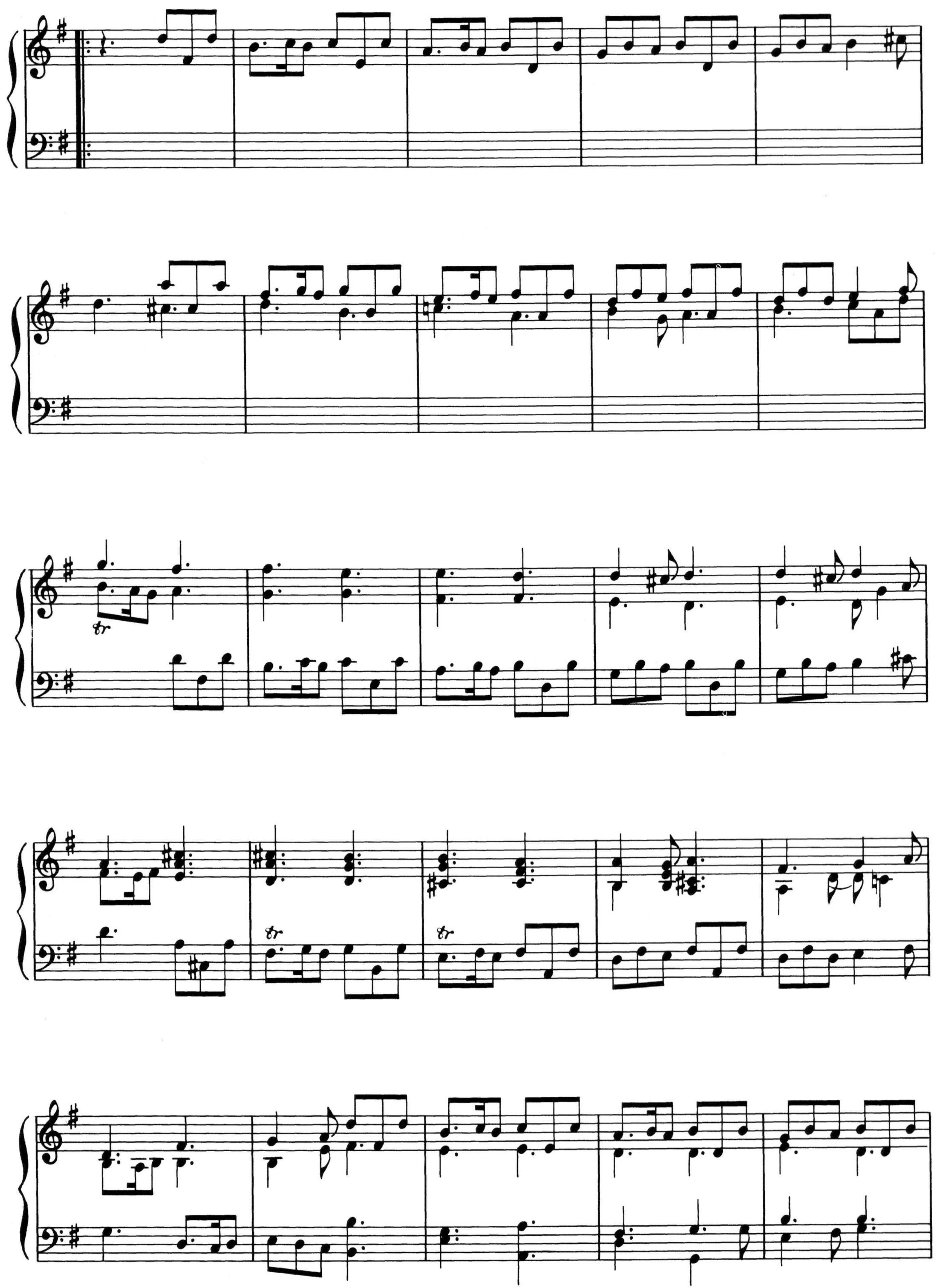

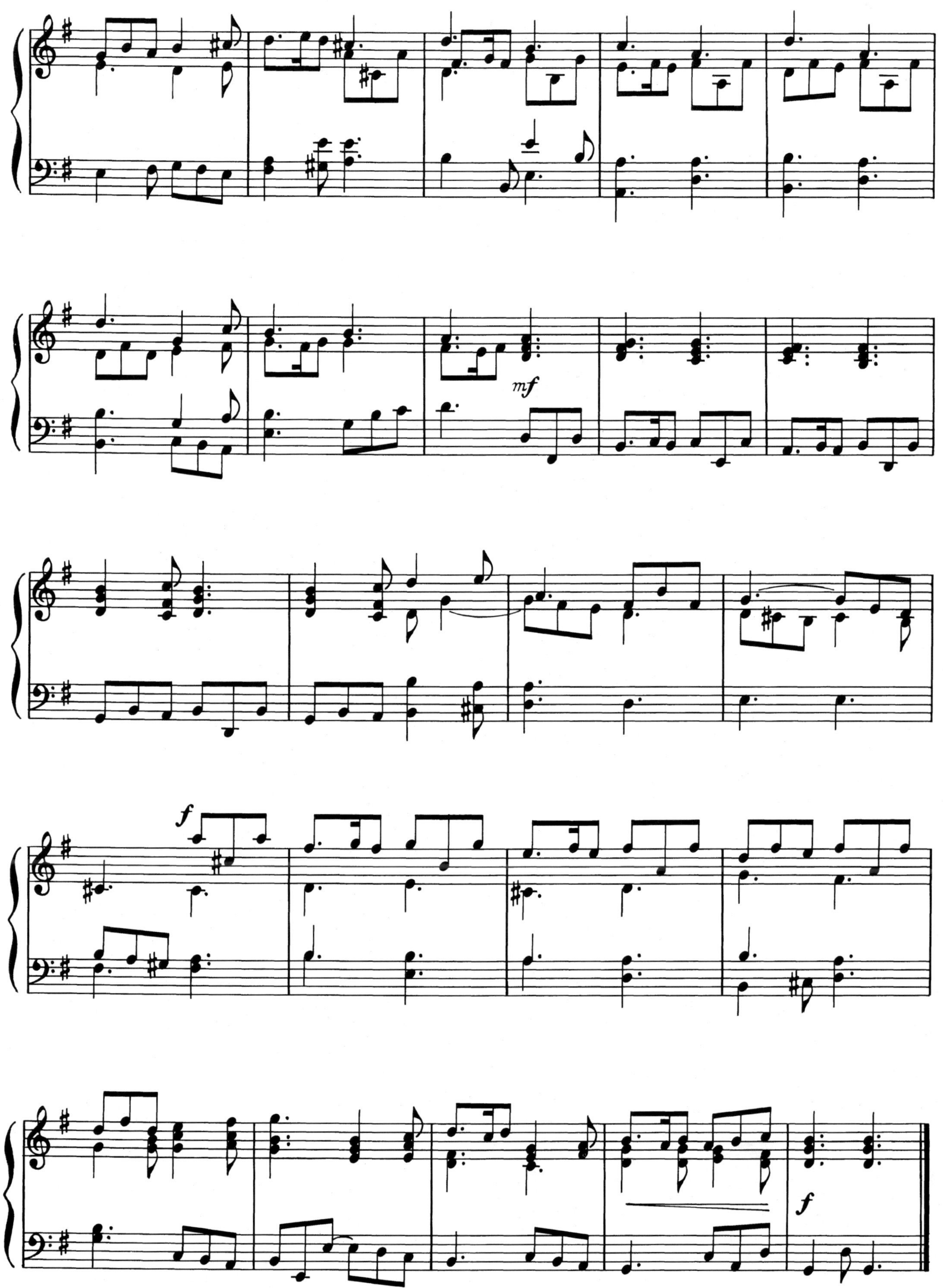

Rest In The Lord

(Goldberg-Variation No. 19)

J. S. Bach
(1685-1750)

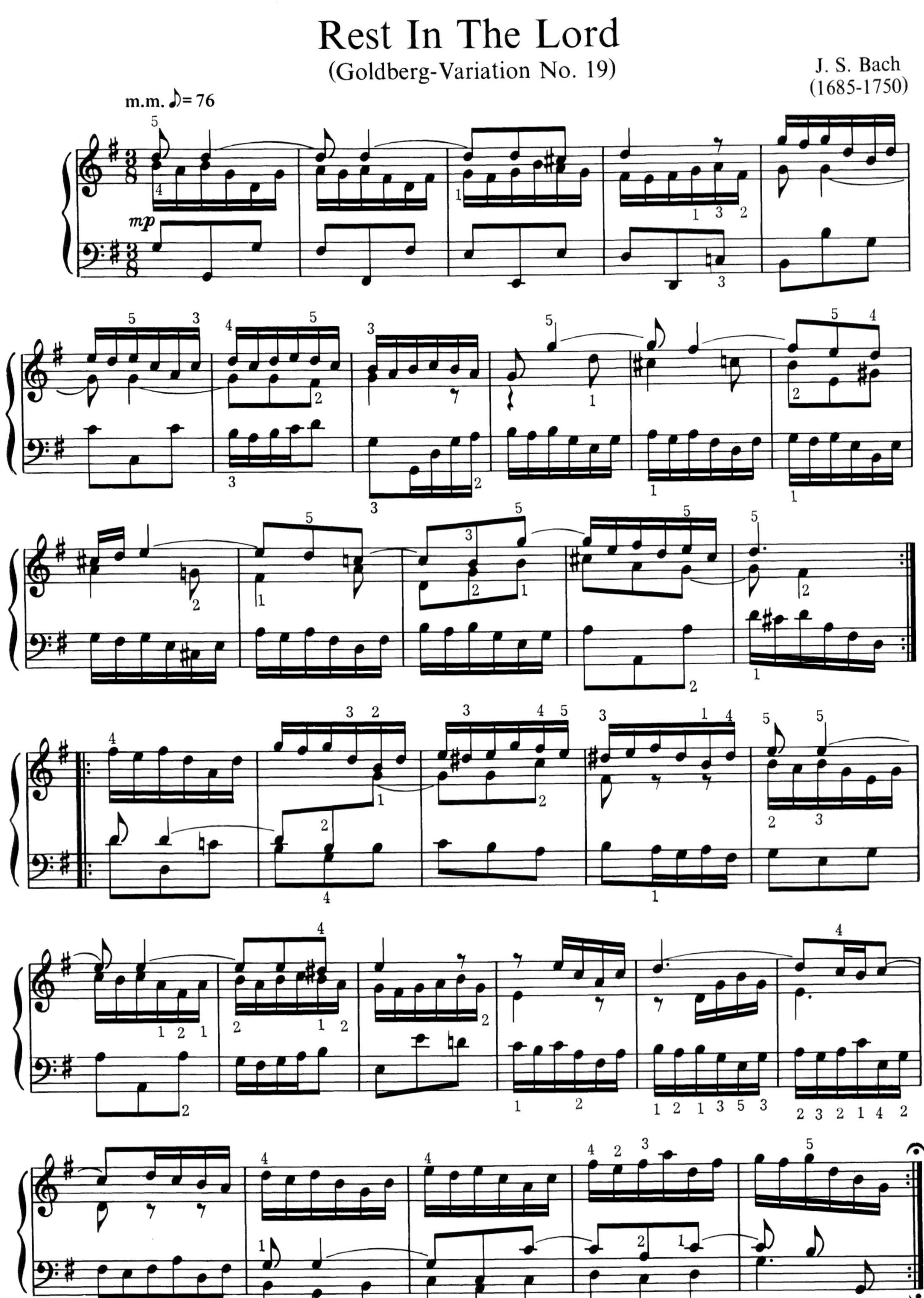

Allemande
(from Suite No. 14)

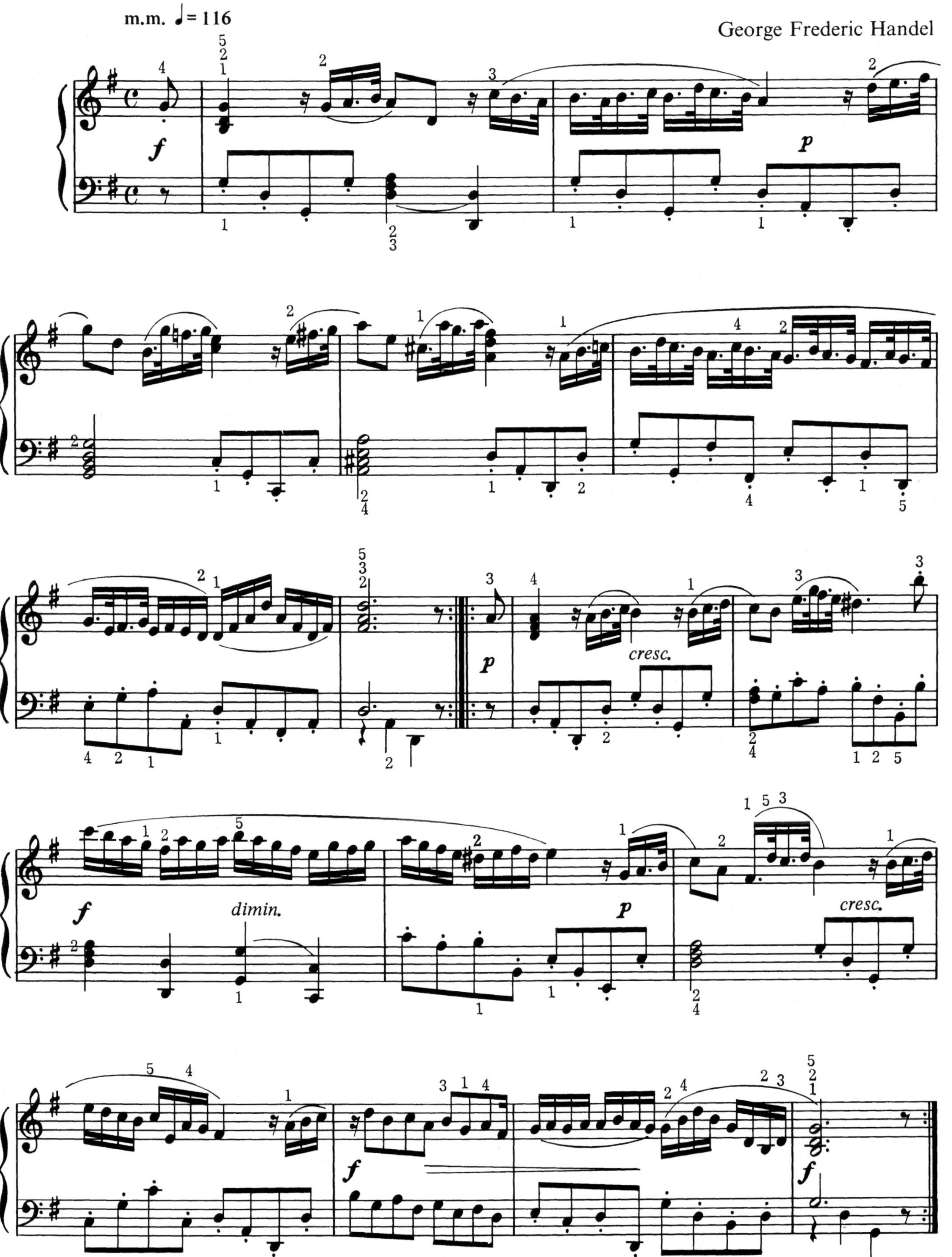

Moments Musicaux

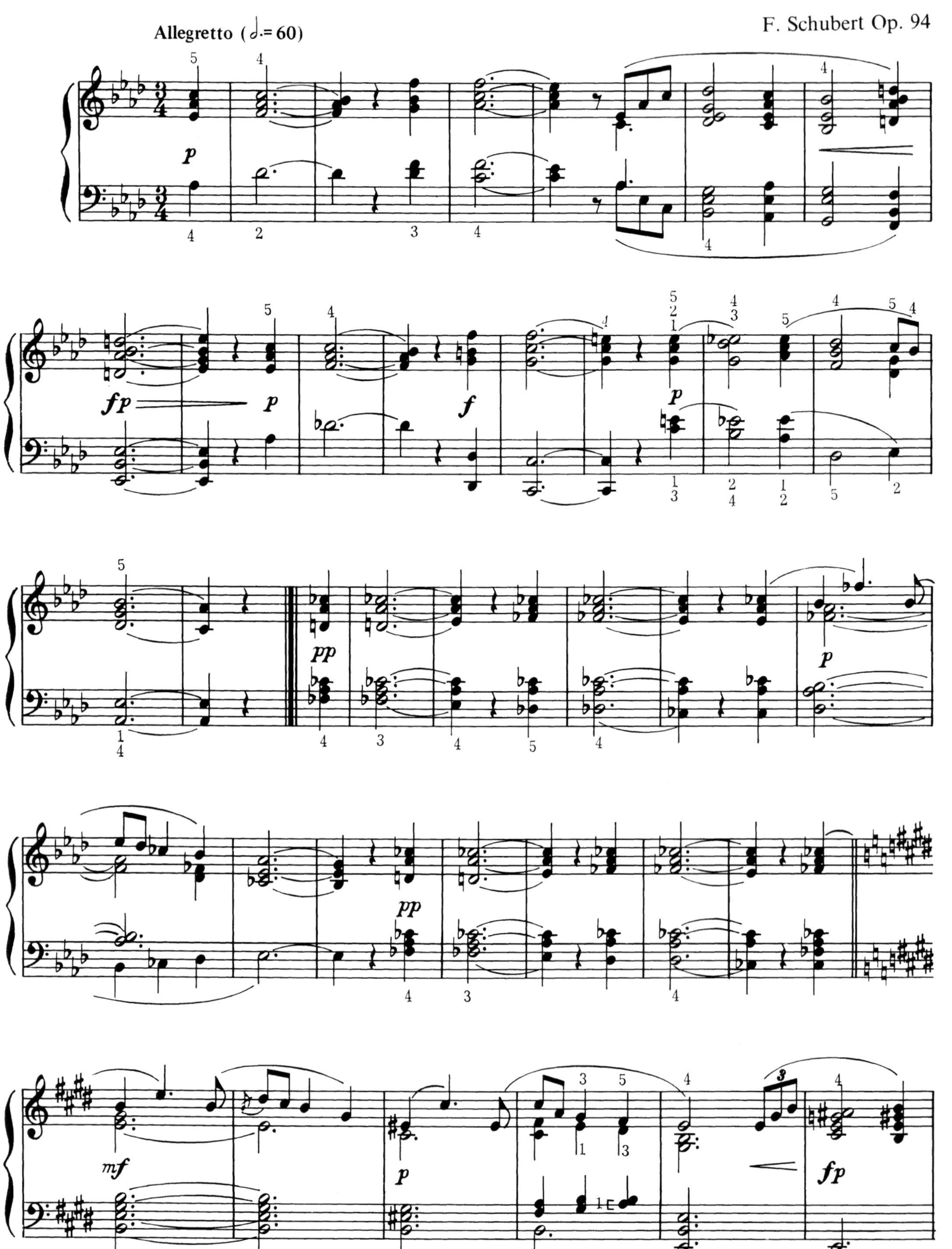

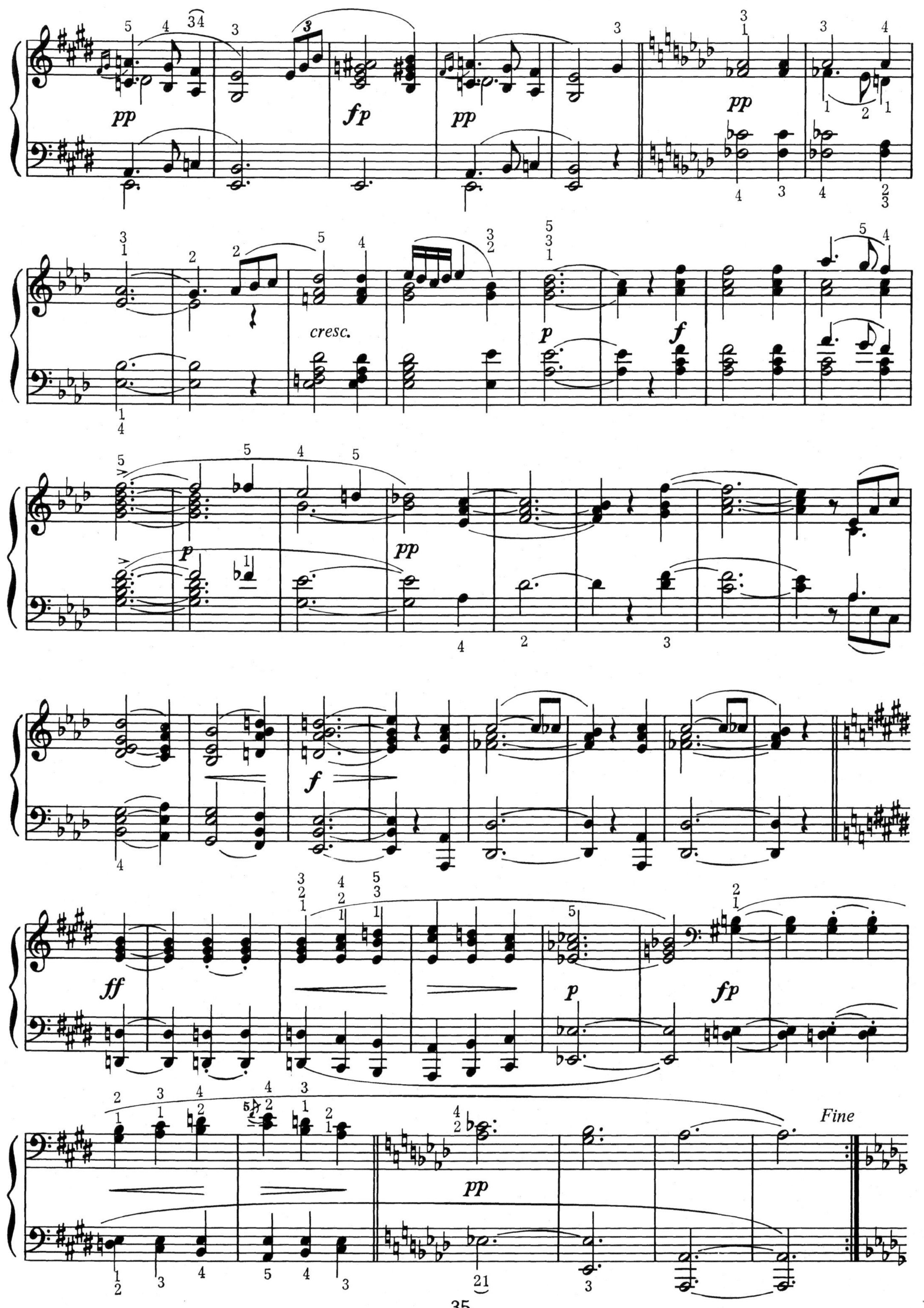

pp
fp
pp
pp
cresc.
p
f
p
pp
f
ff
p
fp
pp
Fine
35

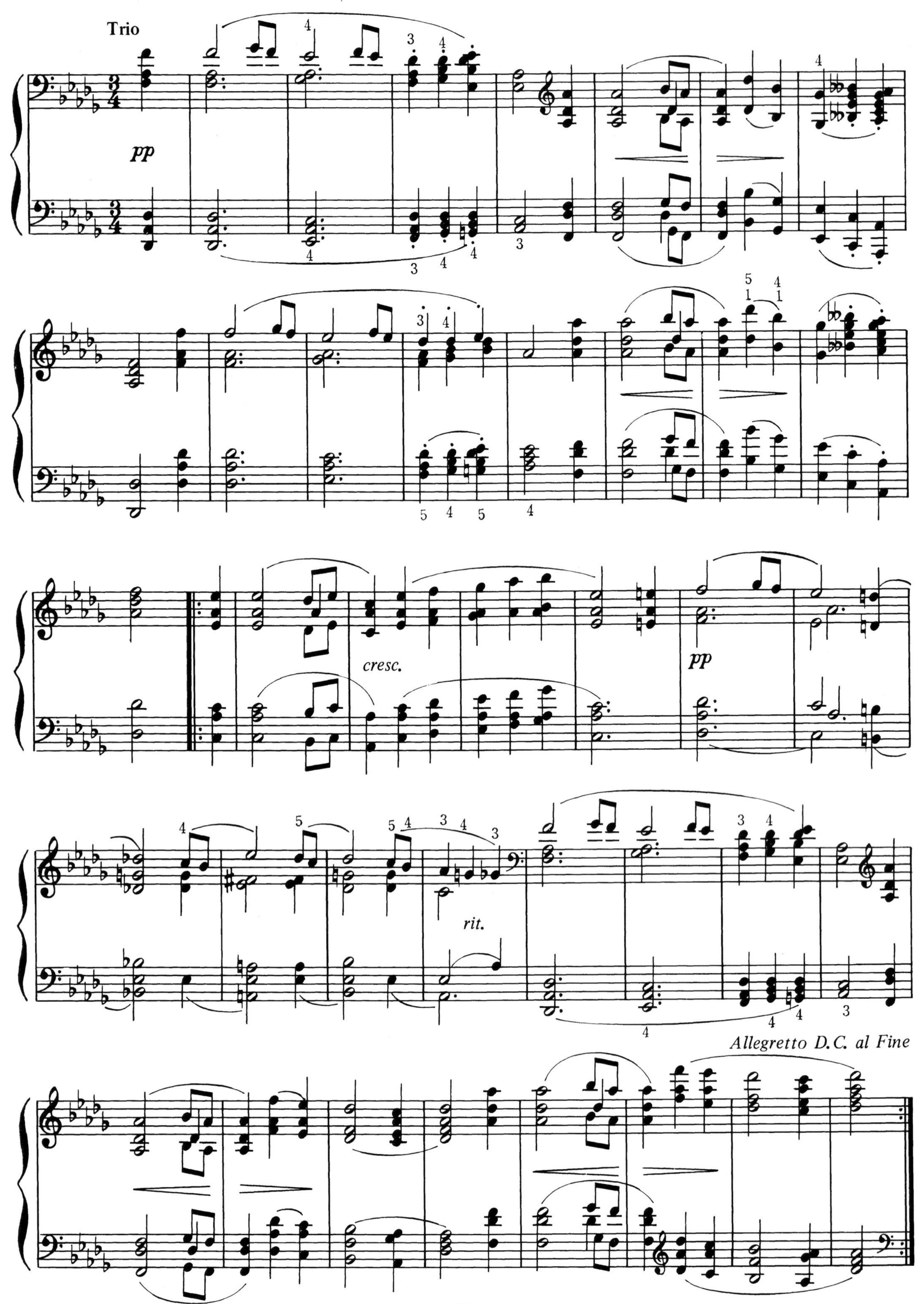

Trio
pp
cresc.
pp
rit.
Allegretto D.C. al Fine
36

Pastoral
(excerpt from Sonata K. 331)

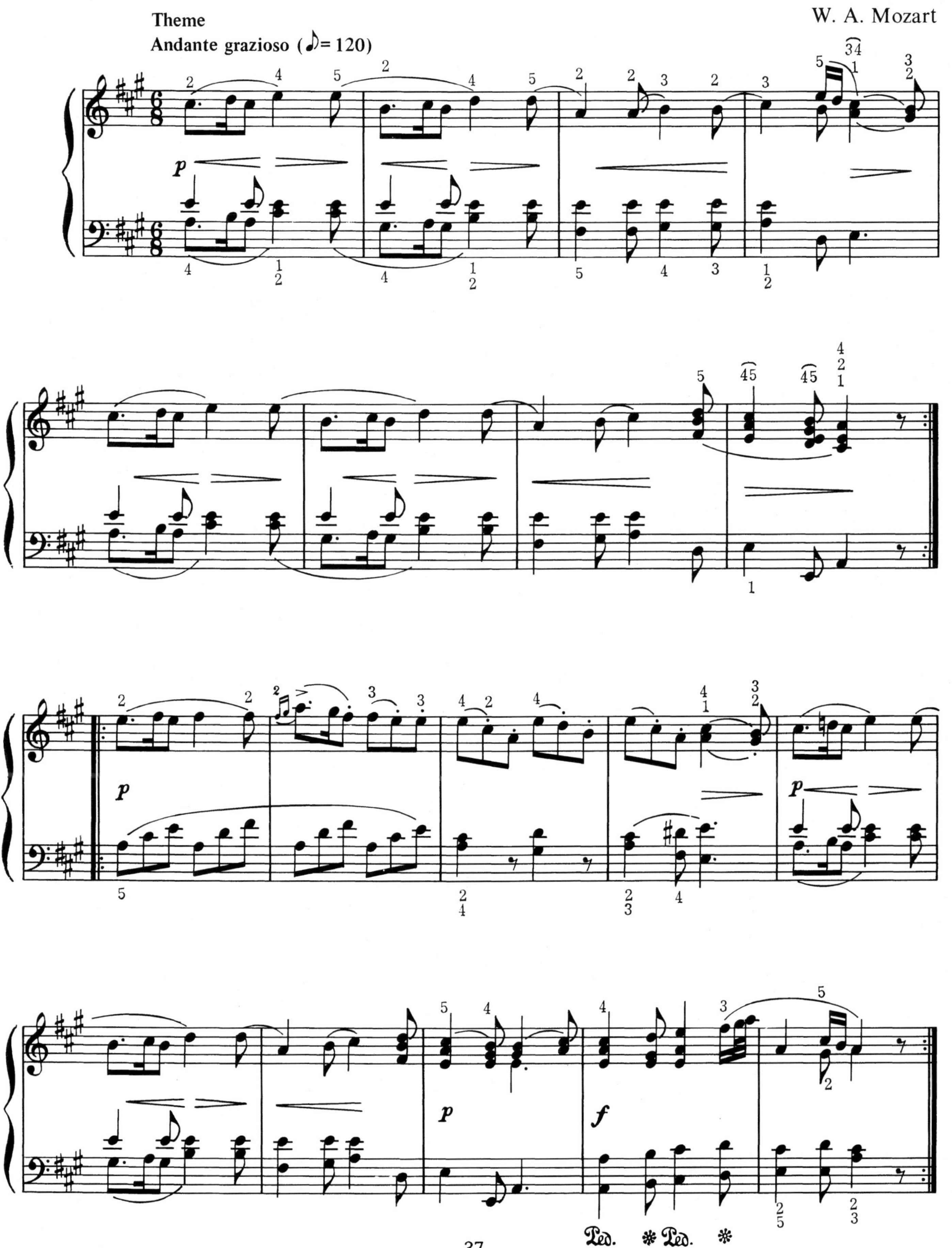

Adagio

(excerpt from "Pathetique" sonata) Ludwig van Beethoven Op. 13

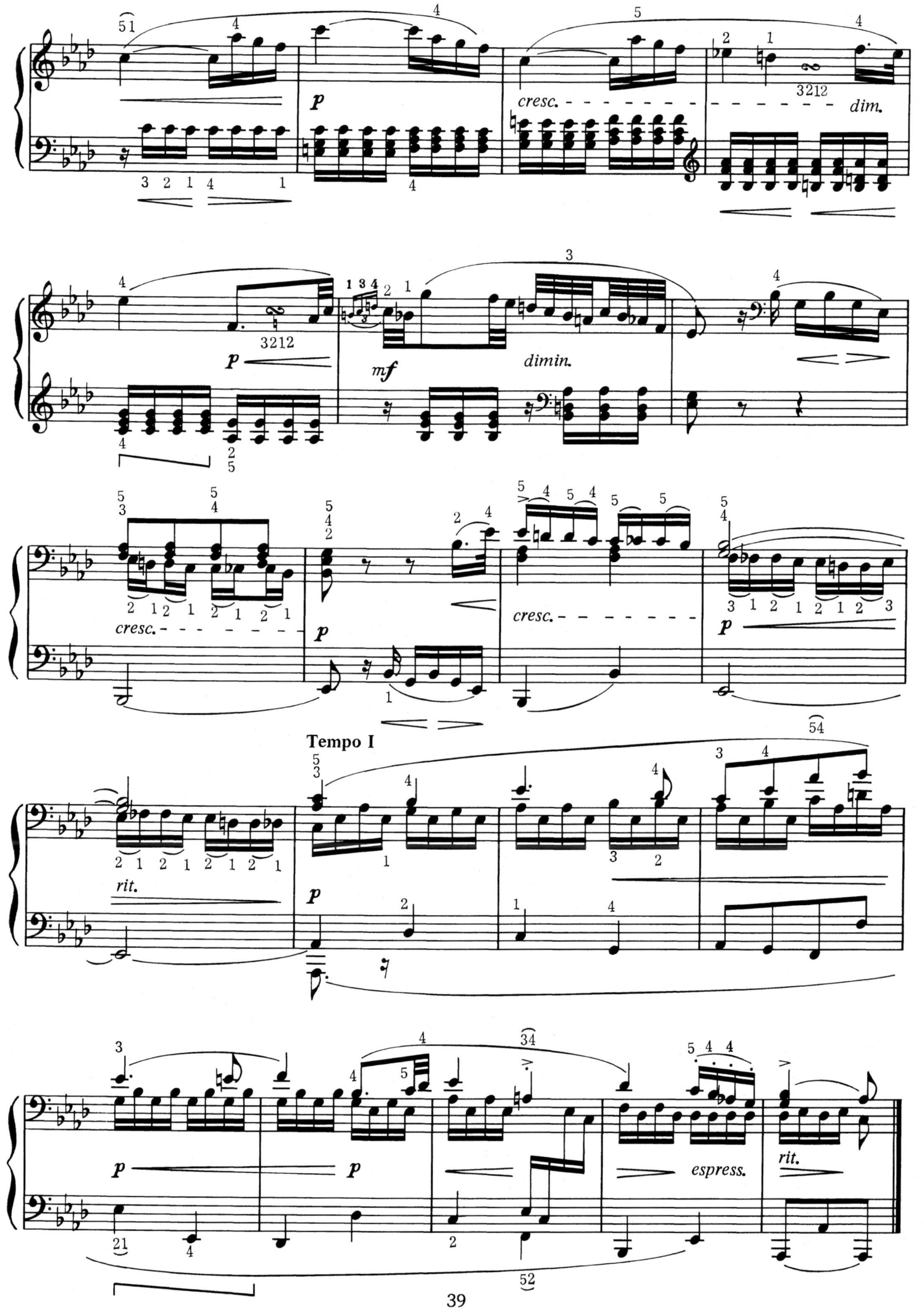

Tempo I
39

To A Wild Rose

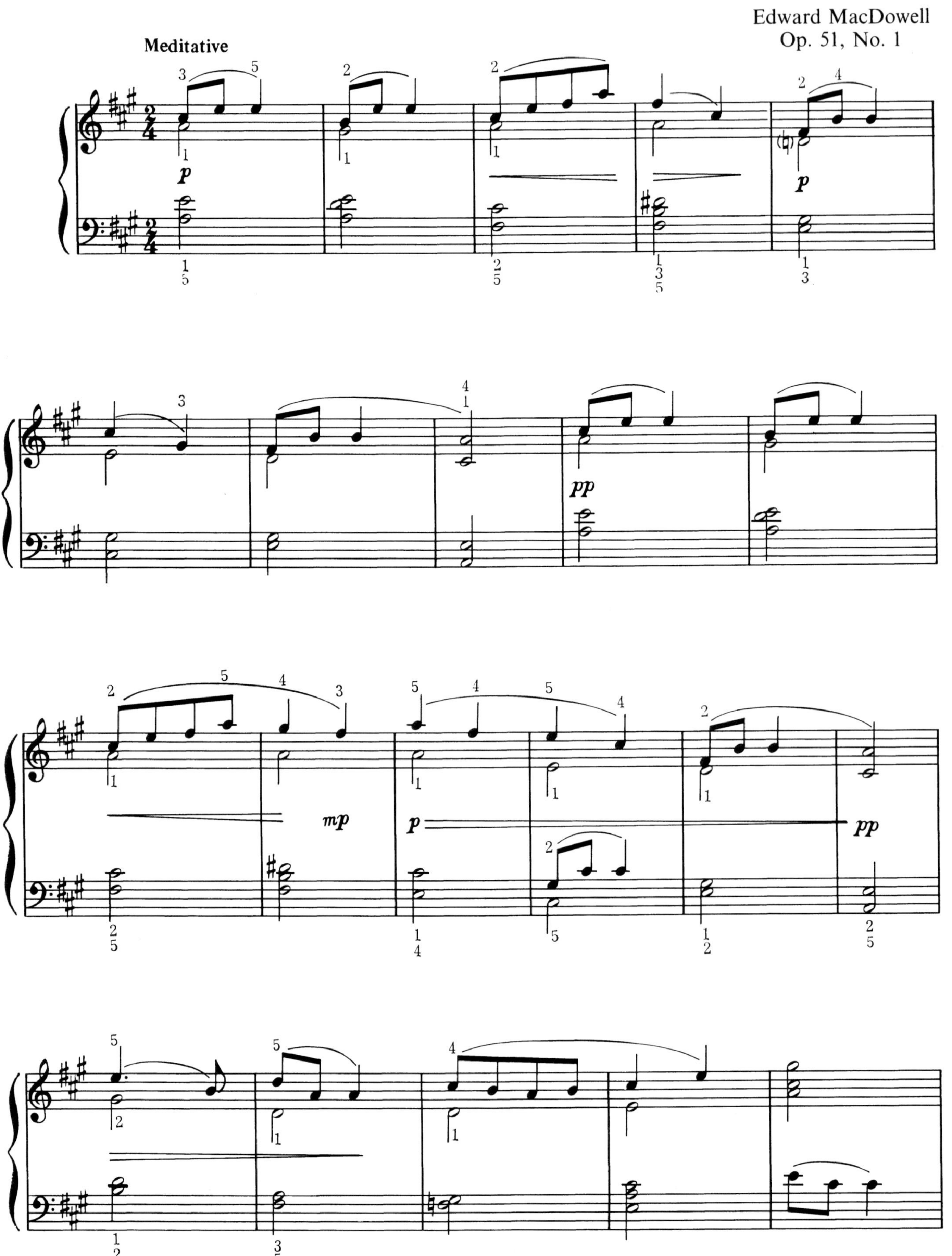

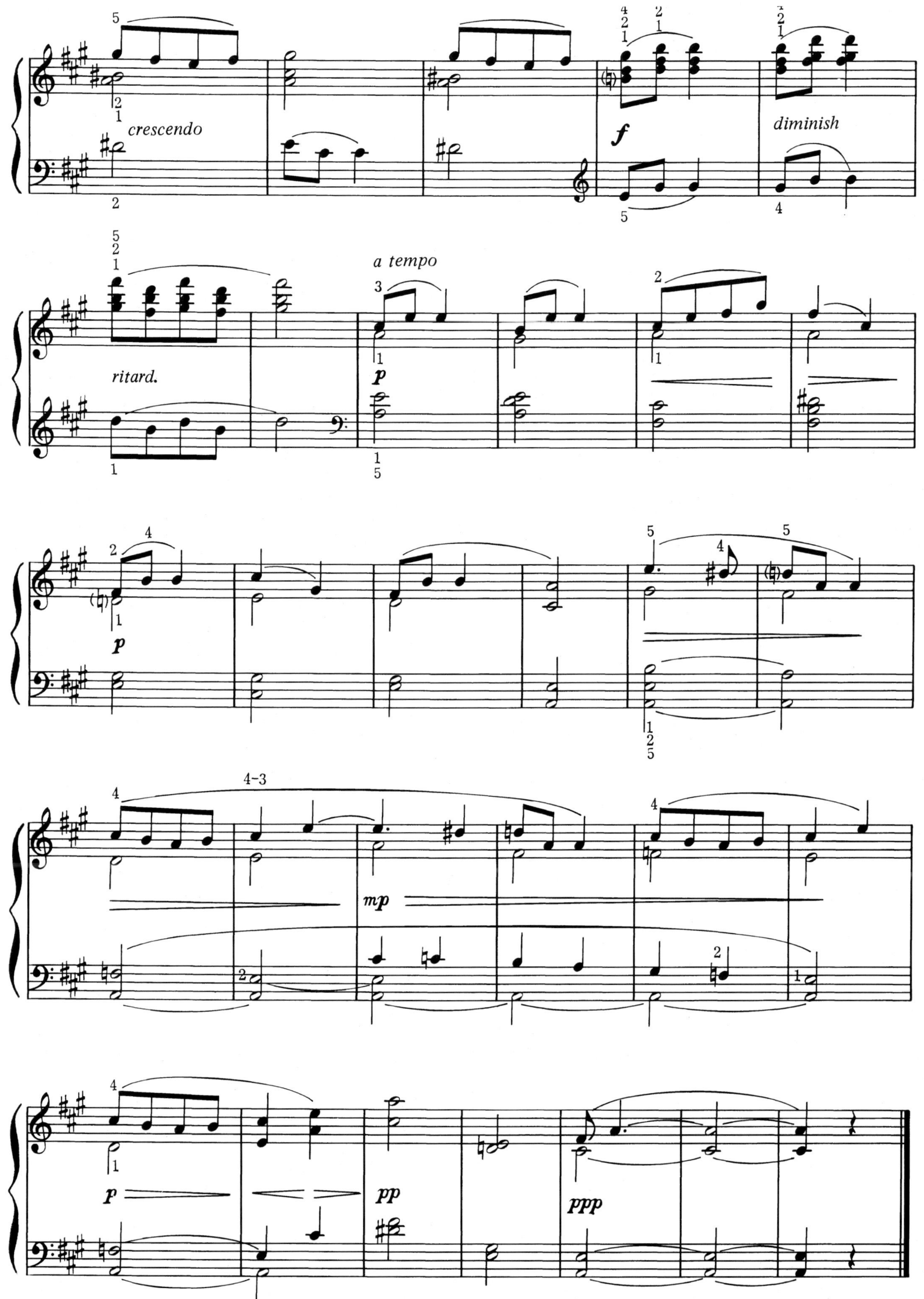

crescendo
diminish
f
5
2
1
2

a tempo
ritard.
p

p

4-3
mp

p
pp
ppp

Prelude In A

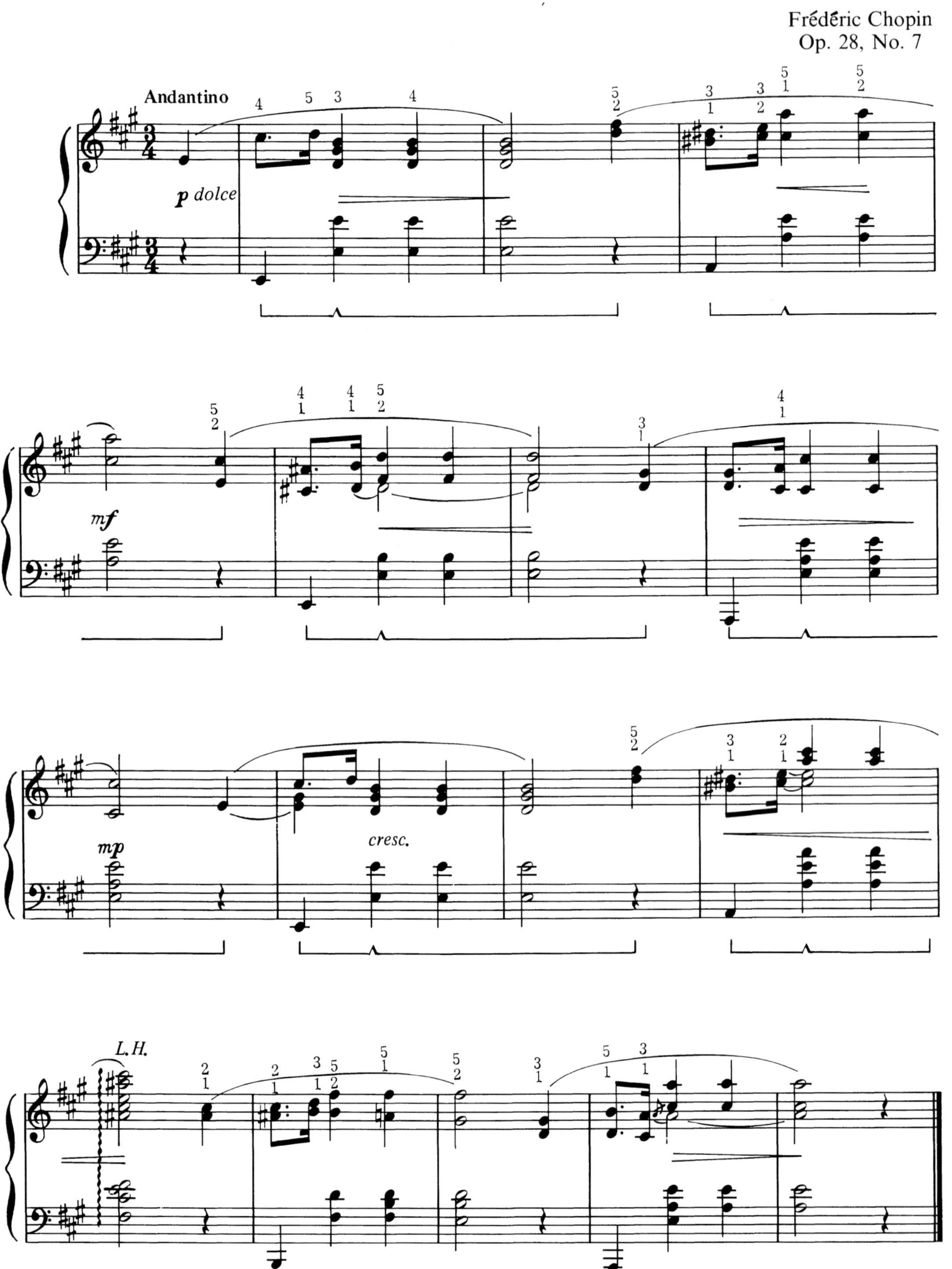

Waltz In A

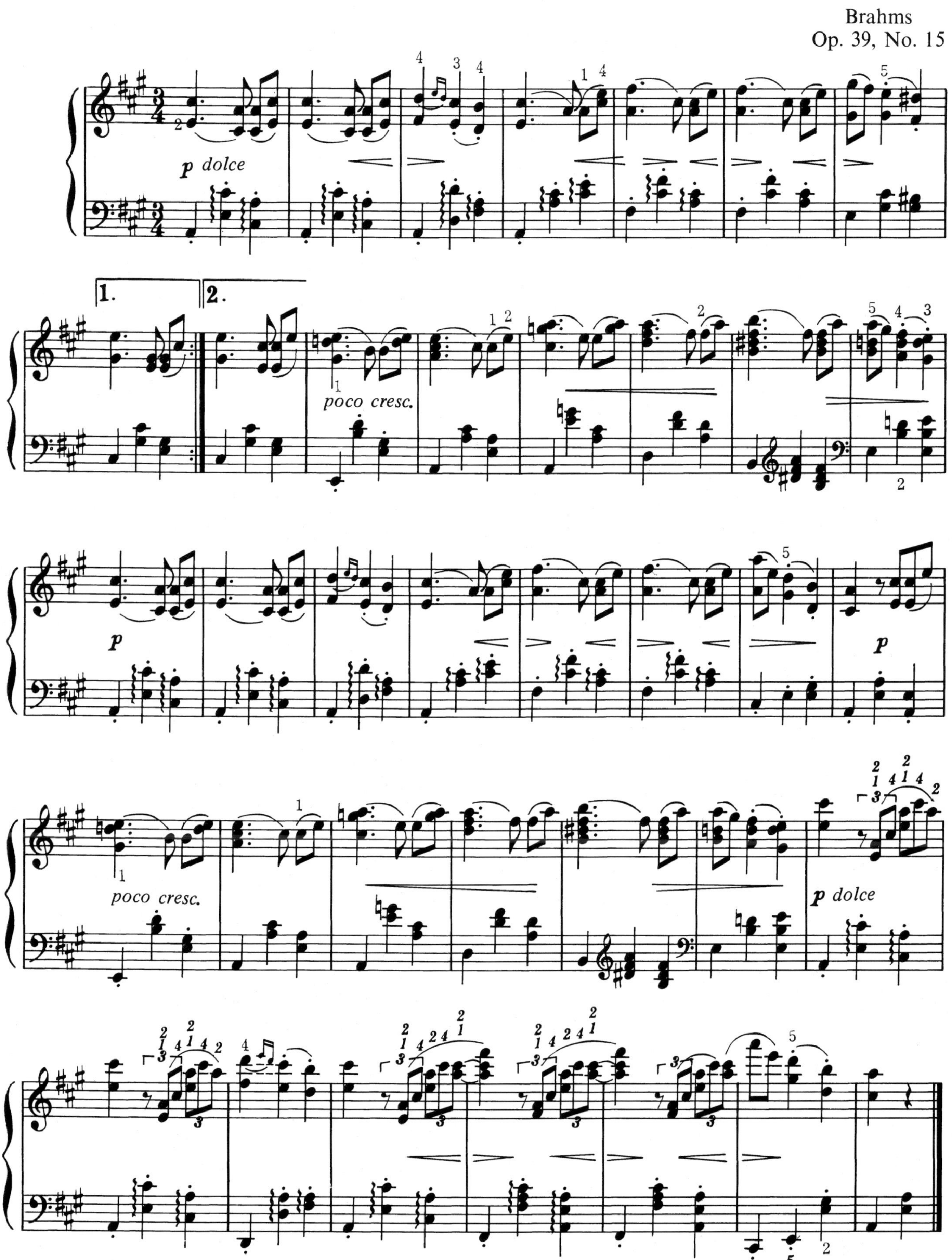

* The original key has been retained.

Song Without Words

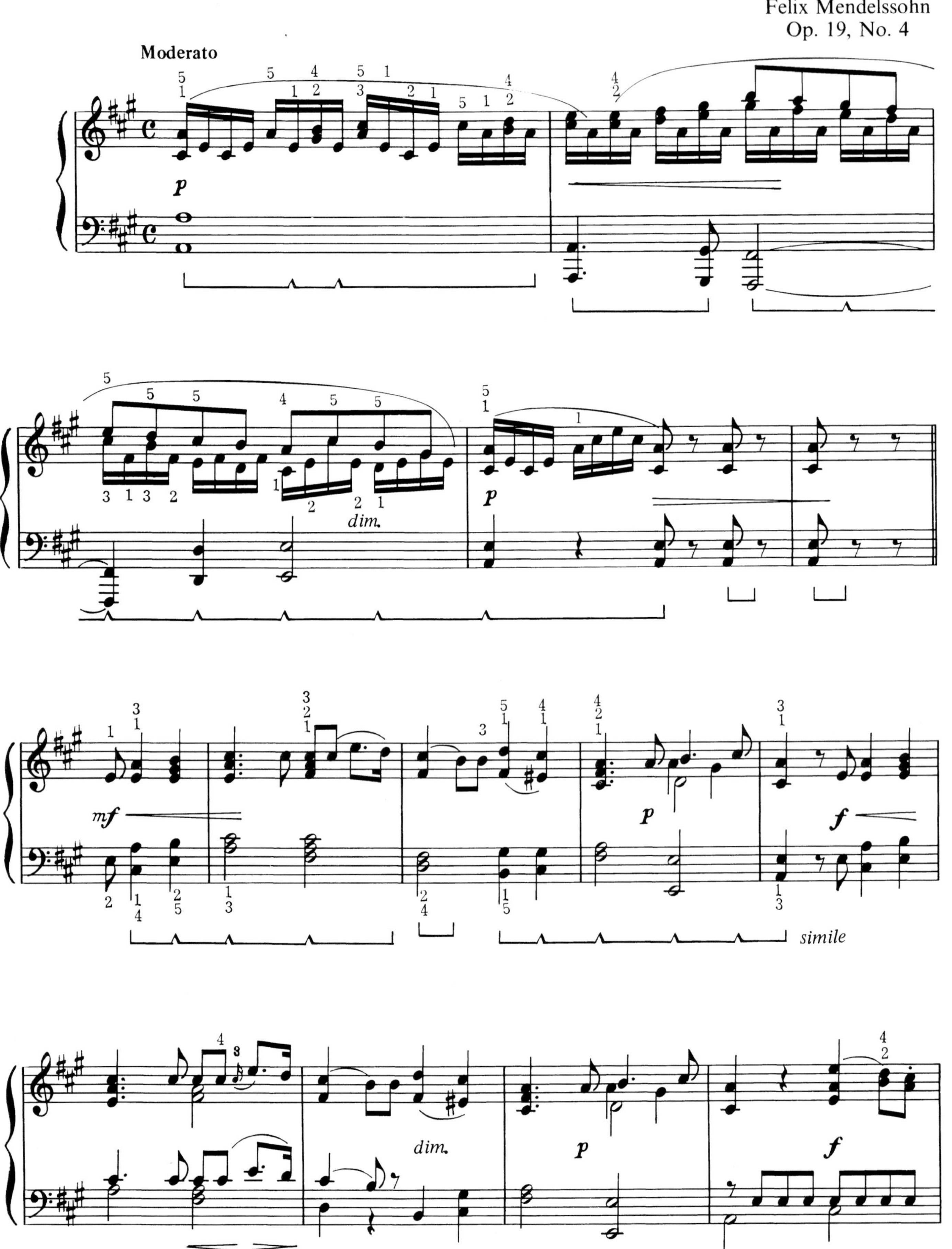

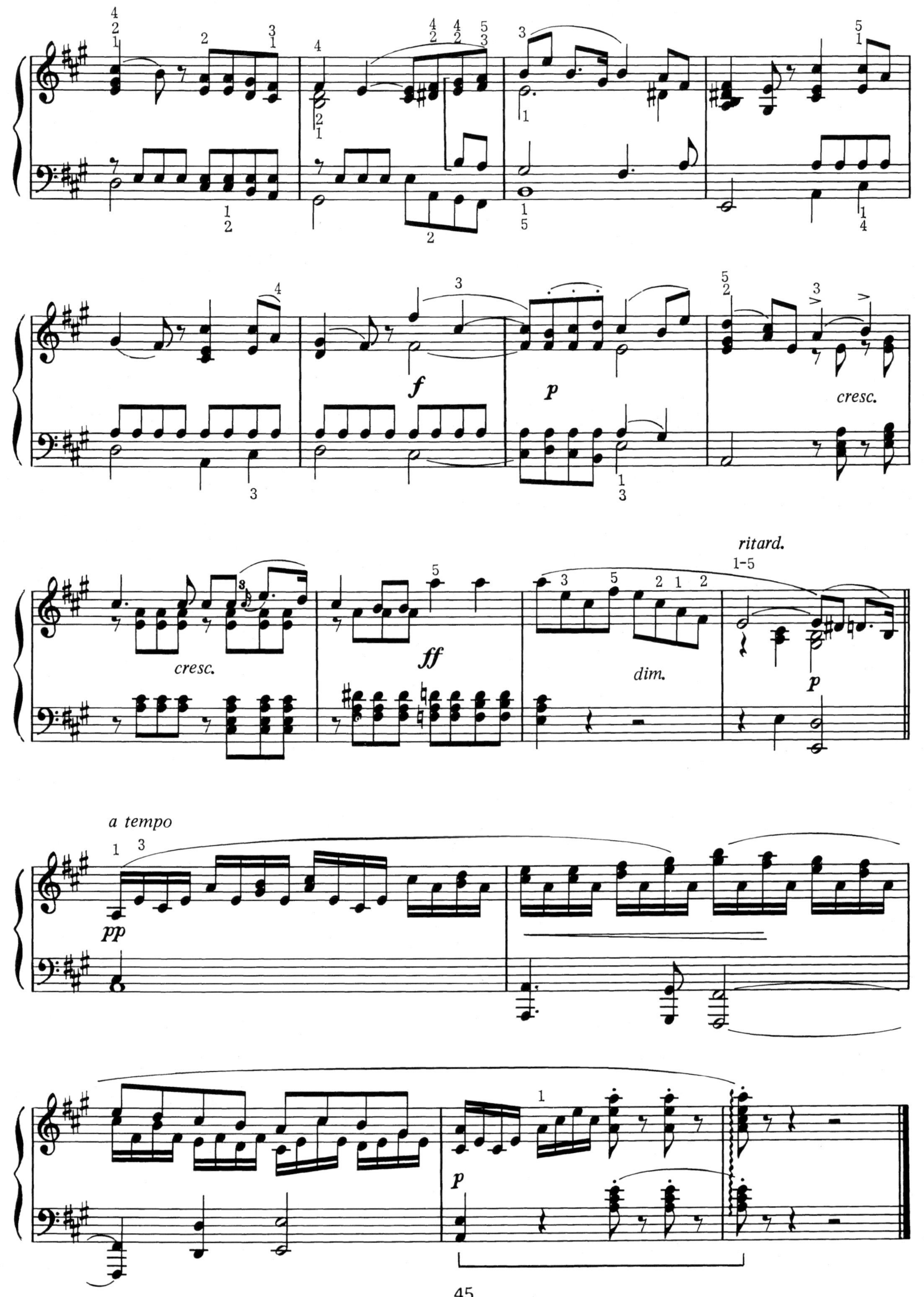

f
p
cresc.
cresc.
ff
dim.
ritard.
p
a tempo
pp
p
p

Rejoice

Gottlieb Muffat

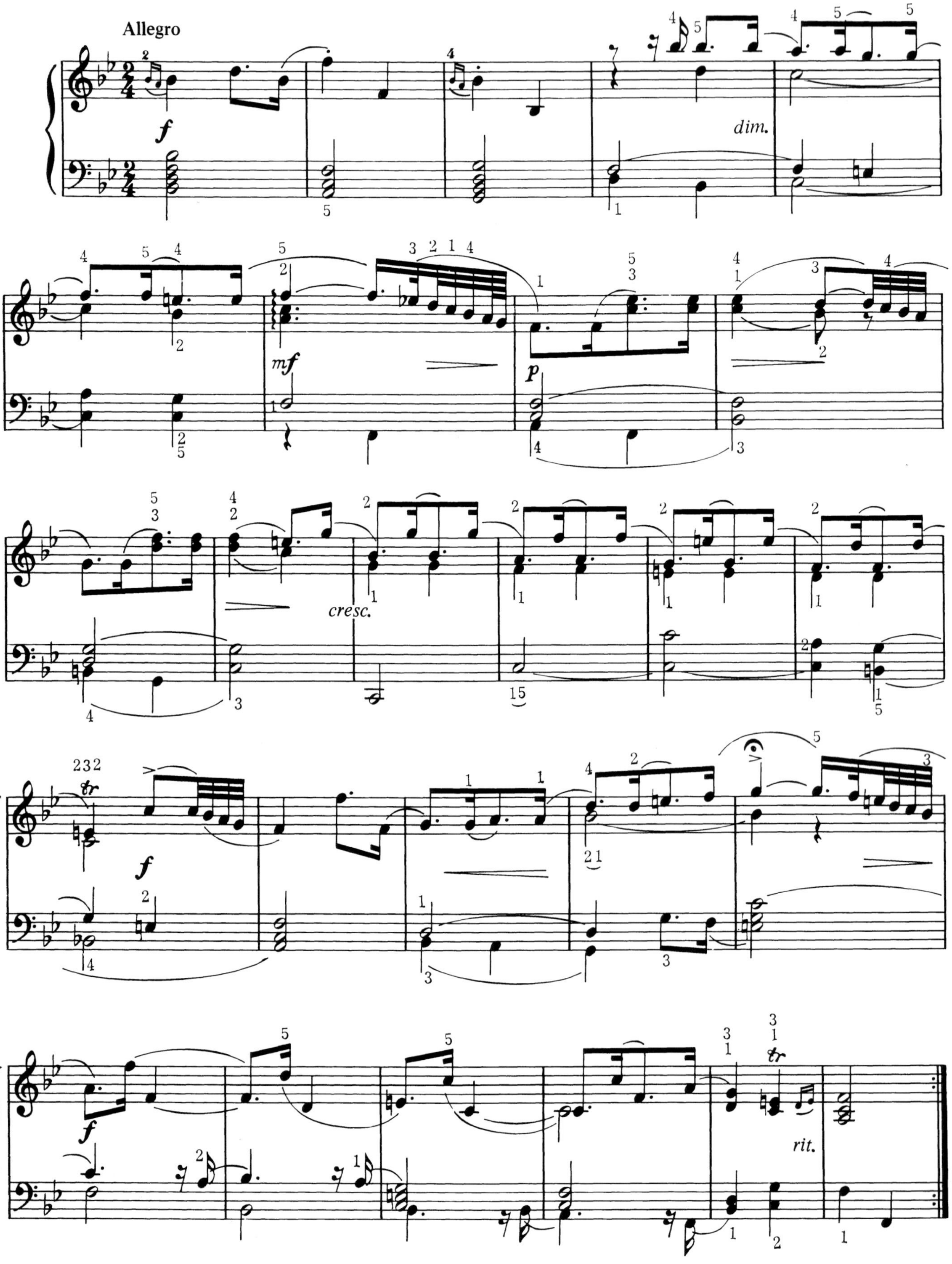

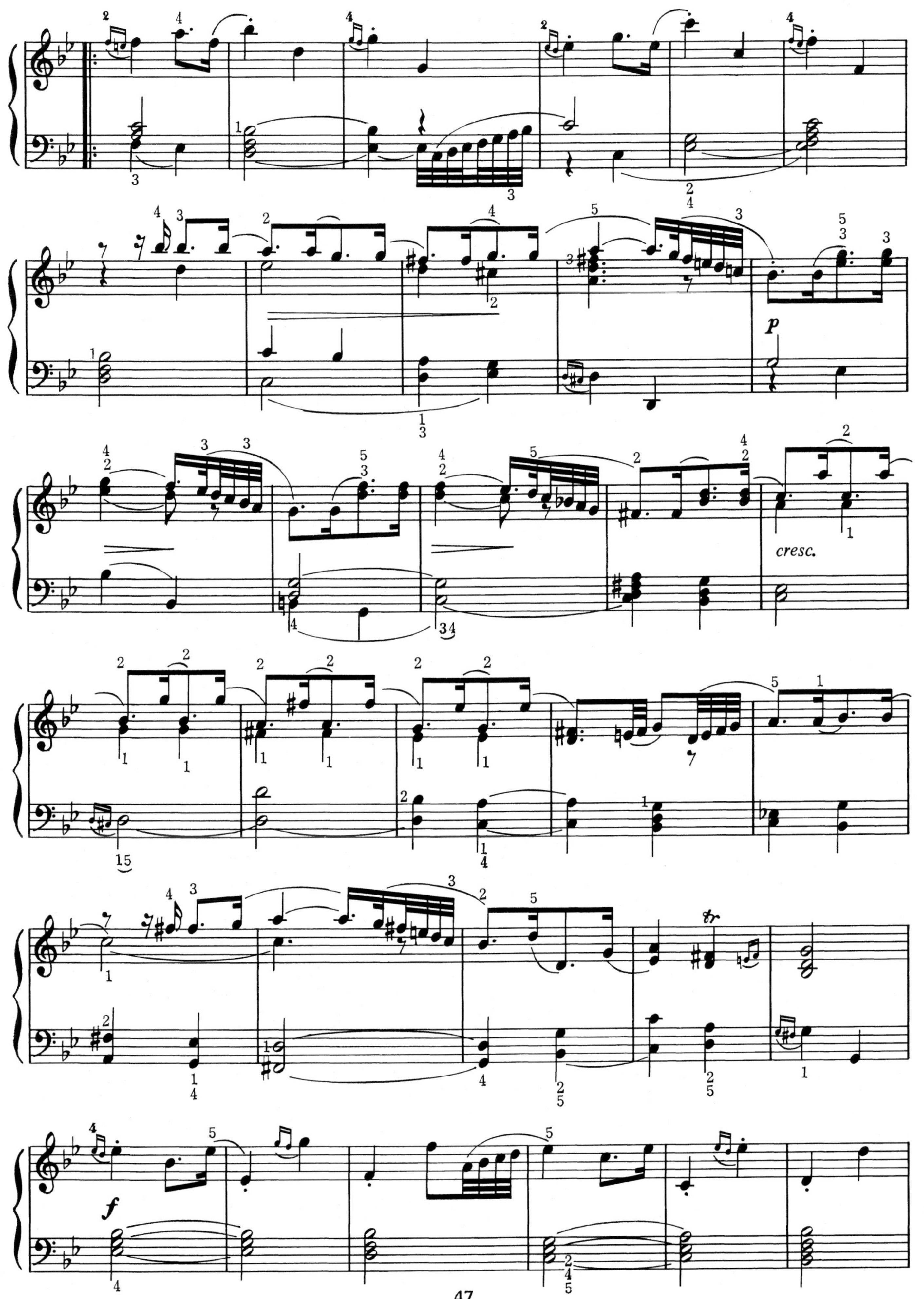

p
cresc.
tr
f
47

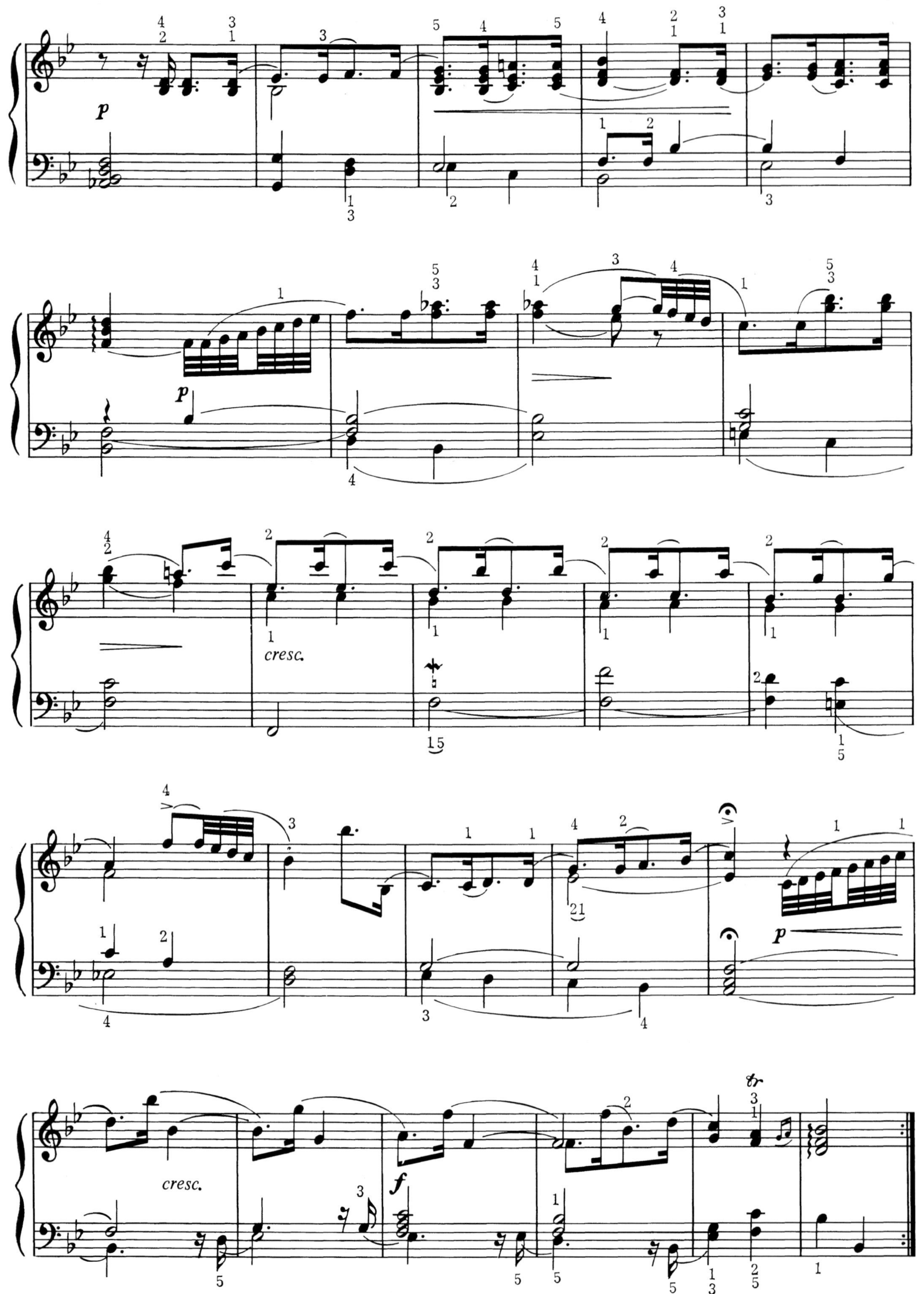

Impromptu

F. Schubert
excerpt from Sonata Op. 142

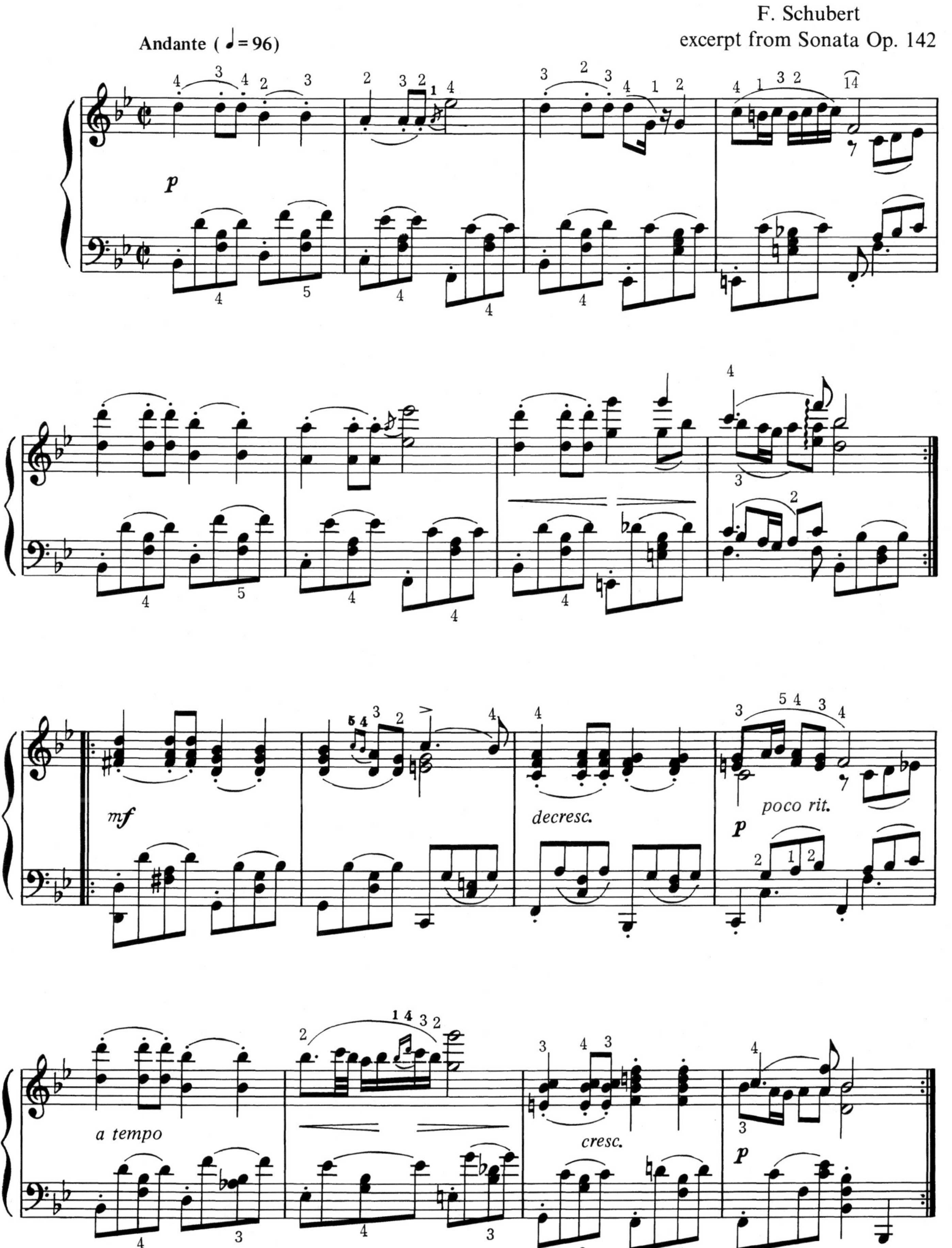

Promenade

(from Pictures from An Exhibition)

Modeste P. Moussorgsky
(1839-1881)

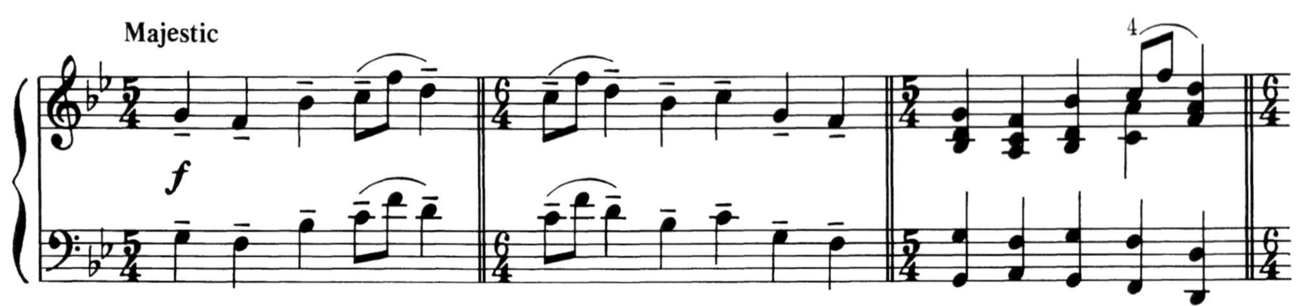

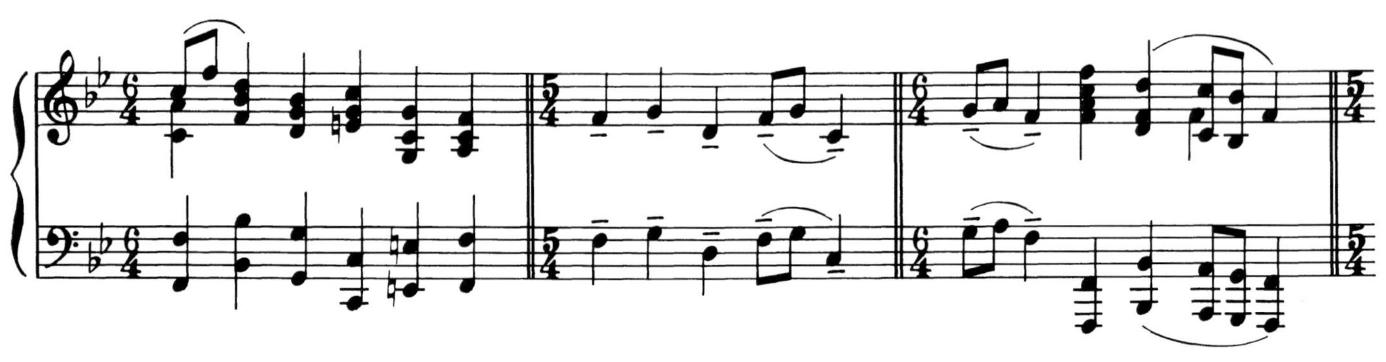

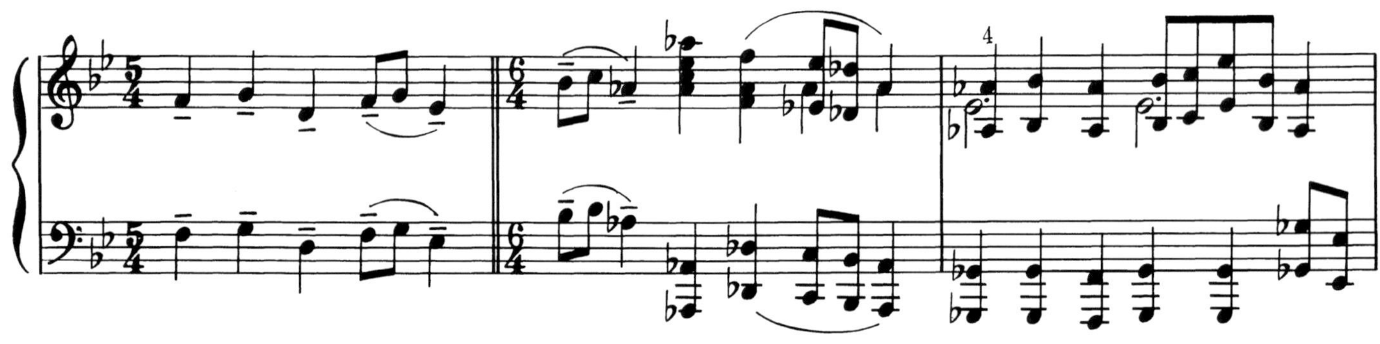

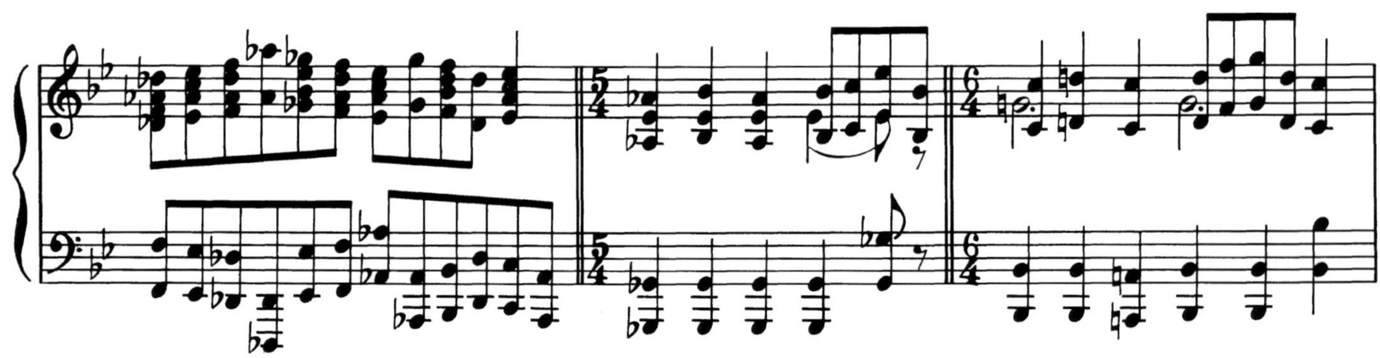

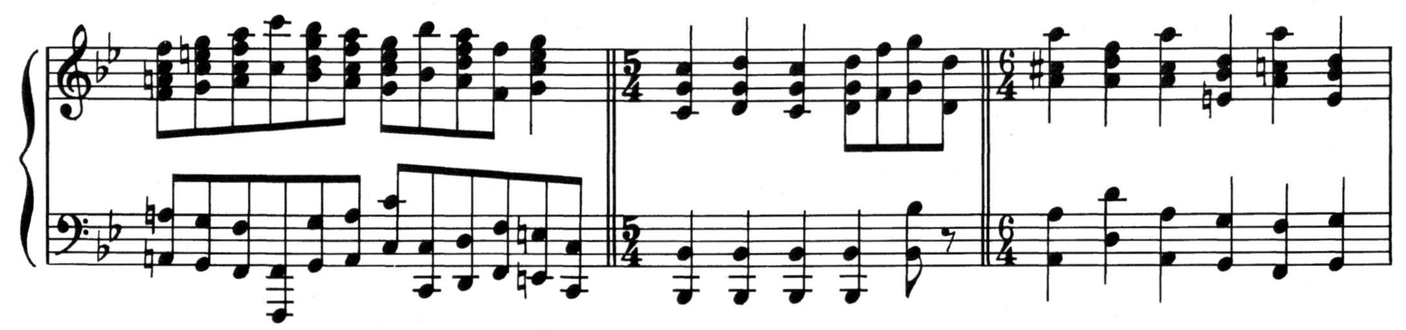

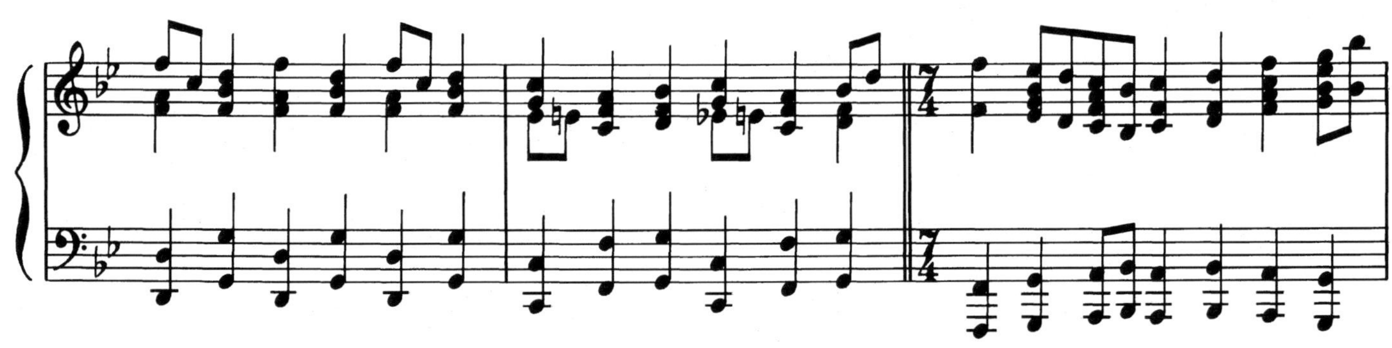

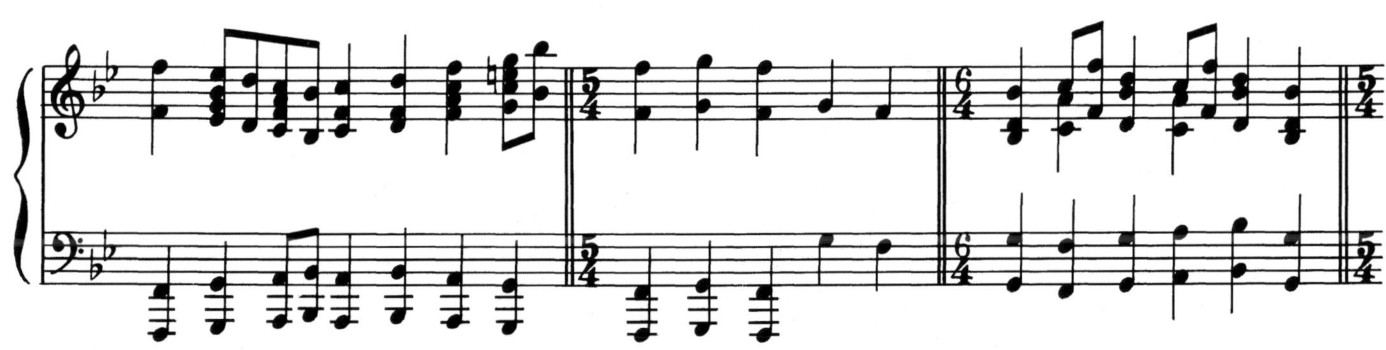

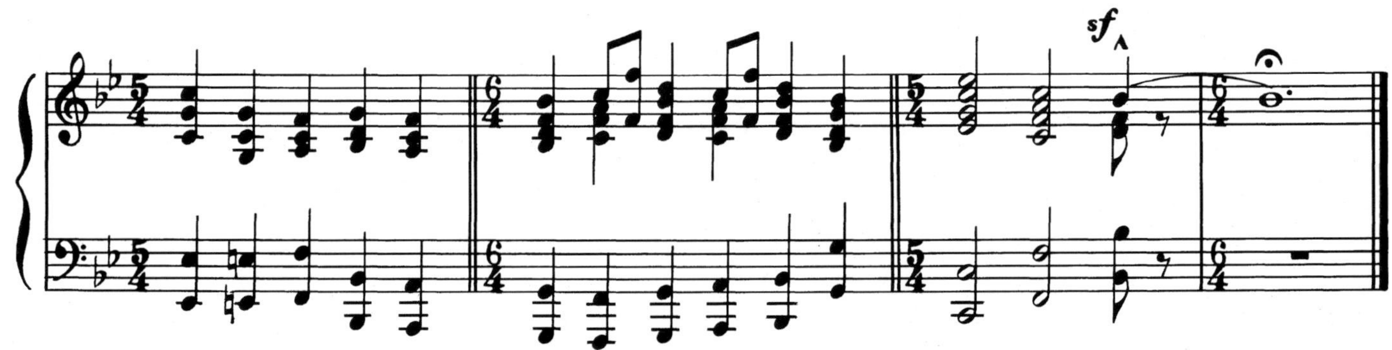

O Sacred Head

(excerpt from Biblical Sonata No. 4)

Johann Kuhnau

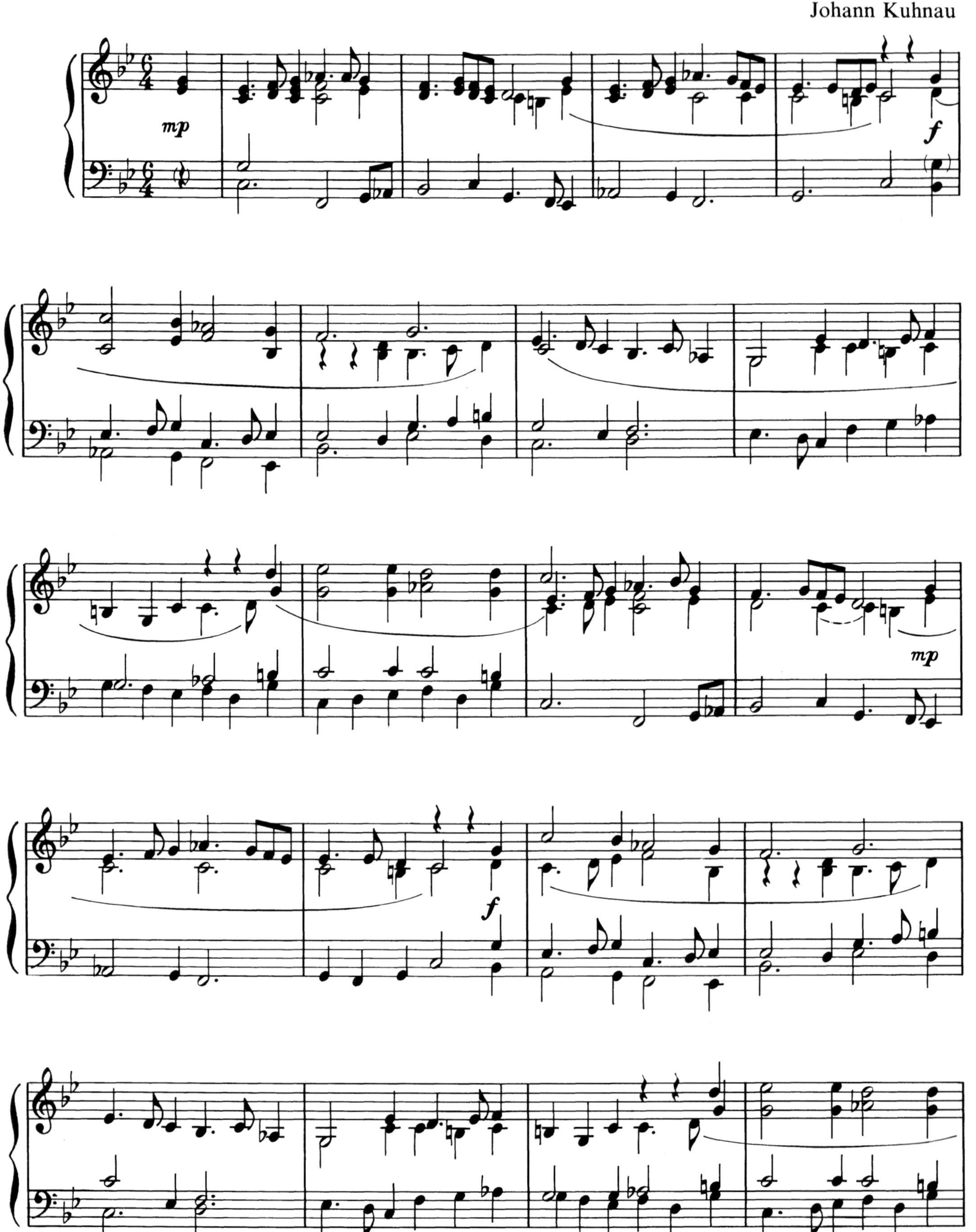

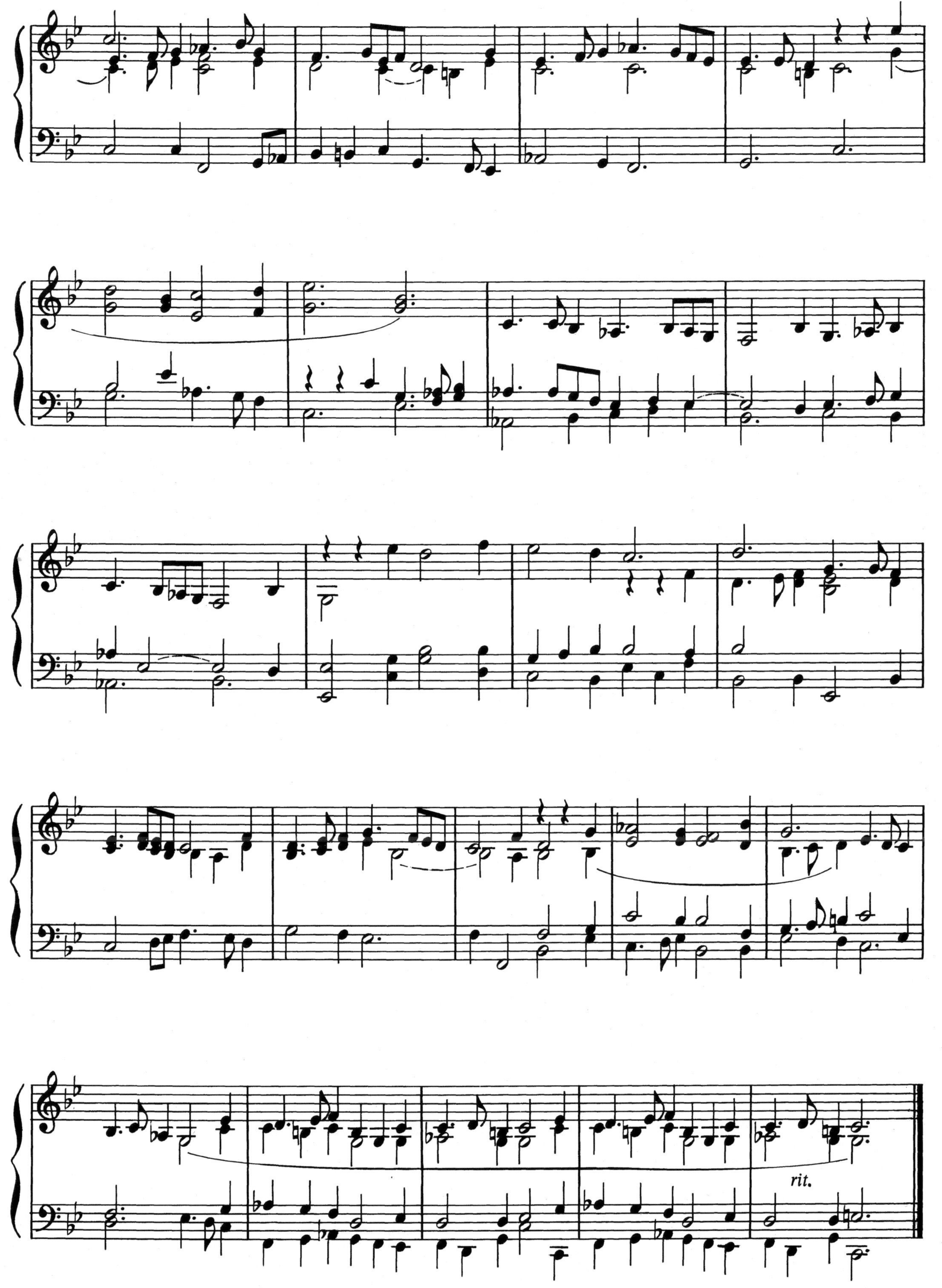

March
(from *Le Prophete*)

G. Meyerbeer

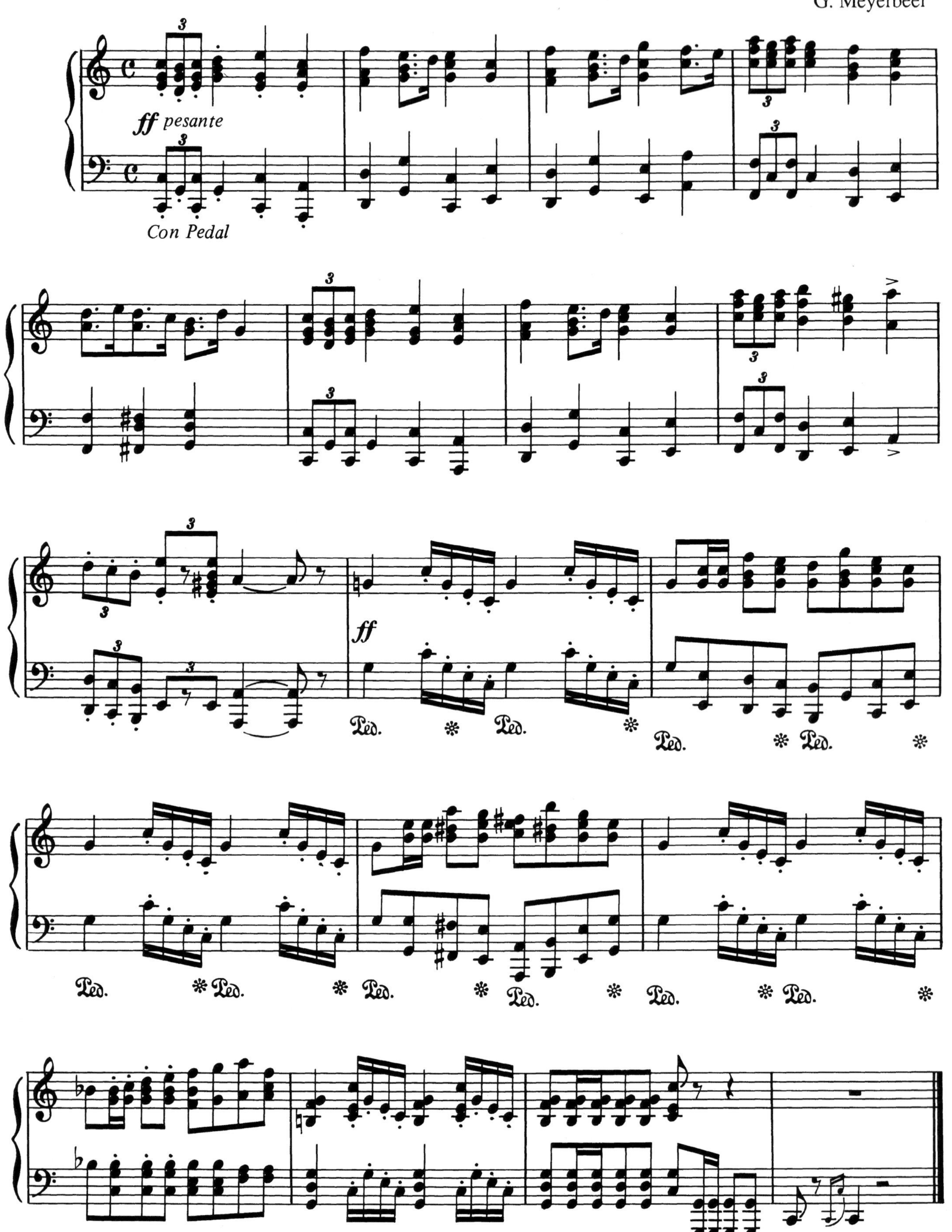

Evening Prayer
(from "Hansel and Gretel")

Engelbert Humperdinck

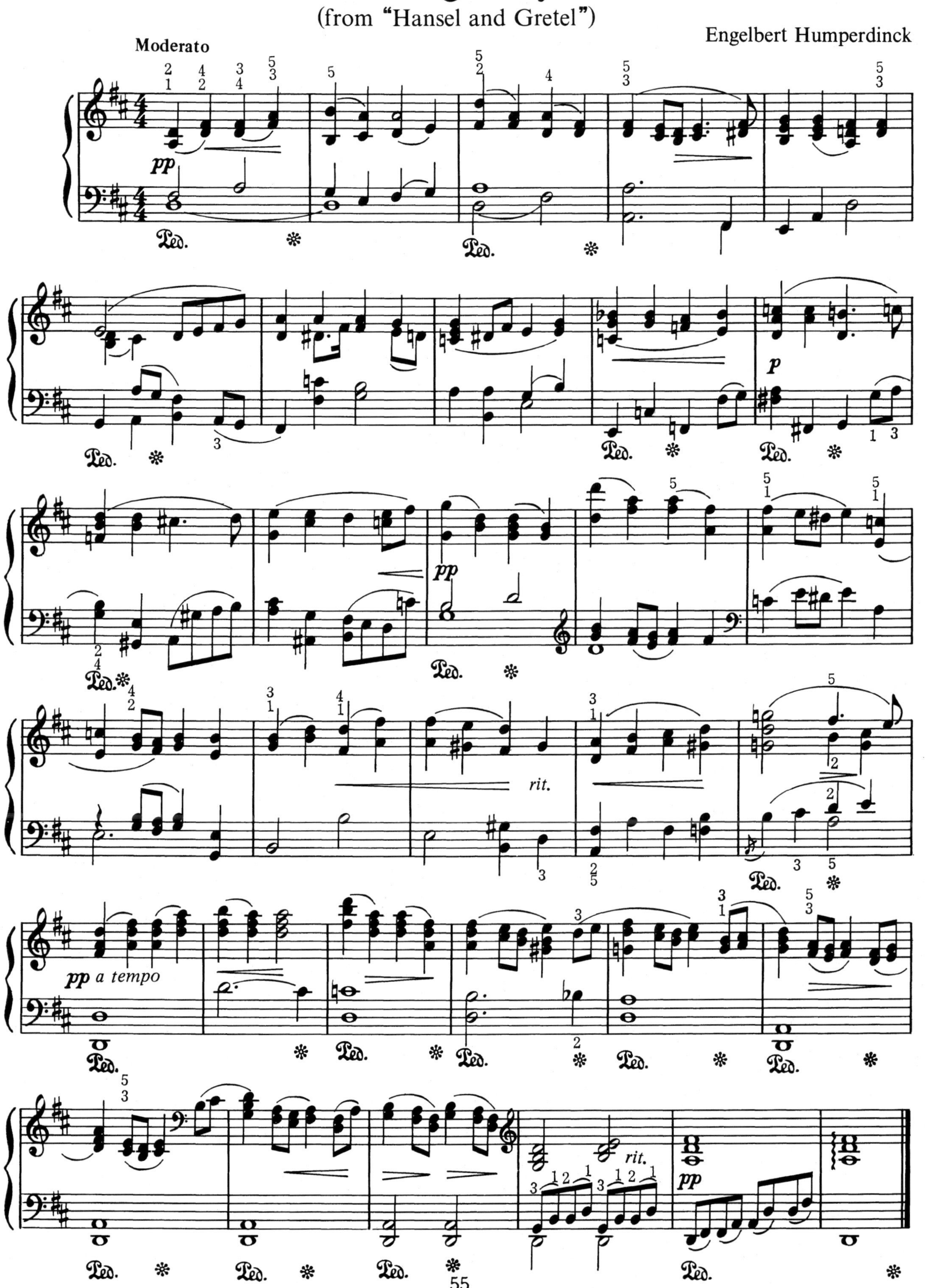

Index

Adagio	*Beethoven*	*38*
Allemande	*Handel*	*33*
Andante	*Gluck*	*11*
At Peace	*Granados*	*10*
Consolation	*Mendelssohn*	*19*
Descend On Us, Holy Spirit	*Mozart*	*20*
Dream Of Hope, A	*Schumann*	*12*
Evening Prayer	*Humperdinck*	*55*
Impromptu	*Schubert*	*49*
Kind Thought, A	*Beethoven*	*18*
Living Water, The	*Heller*	*22*
Lord Speak To Me	*Schumann*	*26*
March	*Meyerbeer*	*54*
Moments Musicaux	*Schubert*	*34*
Morning Prayer	*Gurlitt*	*7*
O Sacred Head	*Kuhnau*	*52*
Pastoral	*Mozart*	*37*
Praise The Lord	*Mozart*	*16*
Prelude	*Sibelius*	*13*
Prelude In A	*Chopin*	*42*
Promenade	*Moussorgsky*	*50*
Rejoice	*Muffat*	*46*
Rest In The Lord	*Bach*	*32*
Sarabande	*Handel*	*14*
Sonata For Sunday	*Scarlatti*	*8*
Song Of Faith	*Kuhnau*	*24*
Song Of Joy	*Kuhnau*	*28*
Song Without Words	*Mendelssohn*	*44*
To A Wild Rose	*MacDowell*	*40*
Waltz In A	*Brahms*	*43*